THE
DYSLEXIC OILMAN
An Autobiography

LES ELLIS

The events and conversations in this book have been set down to the best of the author's ability, although some names and details have been changed to protect the privacy of individuals.

ISBN: 978-87-974013-1-6

Danish Cataloguing Publication Data: A catalogue record of this book is available from The Danish Library.

Also available on Kindle.

Contents

Prologue

I was born on 12th January 1952, one of four boys to Myrtle and Doug Ellis in Newport, Monmouthshire, South Wales, just 12 miles from the capital, Cardiff. I had a troubled childhood, mostly the result of Pink disease, a form of mercury poisoning prevalent in the first half of the 20th century. It affected 1 in 500 children with a hyper-sensitivity to mercury and caused a range of severe symptoms including loss of speech, loss of interest in usual activities, hypersensitivity to light, pain, seizures and, in up to 20 per cent of cases, death. The disease was essentially wiped out when mercury was identified as the culprit and removed as an ingredient in teething powders in the 1950s. From the age of twelve months until I was seven years old, I was prescribed phenobarbital to treat and prevent seizures; I was an addict and I can still remember coming off the drug. Long-term use of phenobarbital is associated with a number of cognitive deficits in adults, including issues with learning and memory. During my time at school, dyslexia wasn't understood as it is today, and it was only later in life that I discovered I ticked all the boxes for this learning difficulty, which caused me problems with reading, writing and spelling. I was always in the lower stream class at school and I moved schools three times because I was unable to settle in; this continued until I went to secondary school.

I left school at 15. The week before, I had to go in

front of a panel of teachers who asked me what I wanted to do with my life. I said I wanted a job that would take me around the world and pay me a lot of money. They smiled and said they thought I should set my sights lower, as it would be difficult to find a job like that with my education.

I had three jobs before joining the oil industry. First, I was a carpet fitter. Then I spent time working for British Steel, before forming my own company at the age of 21, Auto Super Shine Ltd. I employed 10 people and we valeted cars for the three biggest car companies in Newport. The business was profitable for four years but, following a dispute with my co-partner, I decided to dissolve the company. That and a divorce from my adulterous first wife meant I decided to run off to the North Sea oilfields, and this is where my story begins.

Bawden Drilling:
My First Day in the Oilfield

After my divorce from Jacky, there was nothing left for me in South Wales. So I headed up to Aberdeen, where my brother Hadyn was living with his family. He was a professor of psychology at Aberdeen University and, through one of his ex-students, he had been able to get me an interview with Bawden Drilling, a Canadian outfit and one of the largest oil drilling companies in the North Sea, with seven rigs.

The interview was easy enough. The personnel manager, Robin, said, "Well, I see you don't have two heads, so all you've got to do now is pass the medical and the job is yours." The day after the medical I started working in the Bawden pipe yard, cleaning drill pipes and bundling them together with thick wire ropes, ready to be lifted into cradles and later put onto a supply boat and taken out to the platforms.

On my first Friday afternoon, Robin came into the yard and told me I would be going offshore the following Monday. This was great news because I would work 14 days offshore, with all my food and accommodation paid for, and then get 14 days onshore, during which time I could go anywhere. Robin told me to report to the railway station at 6.30 am on the Monday morning. There I would join a crew of people from Bawden waiting to go to the Piper Alpha platform. A minibus would pick us up and take us to Dyce heliport.

Pumped up, I hardly slept the night before. I arrived at the railway station early on Monday morning. There was only one person waiting there, a young guy in his early 20s, so I approached him and said, "Do you work for Bawden Drilling – and are you going to the Piper Alpha? "Yes," he said.

"Have you worked there before?" I asked.

"Yes," he said again. "Yes, I've been out before."

"So what's it like?"

"Well, you know, it's quite a dangerous place," he said. "A lot of accidents. During my last trip there was a guy who had an accident with a piece of drill pipe falling on his leg. It was lucky that the rig welder was working nearby and he was able to cauterize the deep cut; it was pumping out lots of blood."

This sounds like a crazy place, I thought. "Does this happen a lot?" I asked him.

"Oh no, not all the time," he told me. He went on to say that there are over 800 people working on the platform at any one time. "You've got the drilling crews and then you've got all the bears." The bears were the civil engineering contractors who slept on two semi-submersible hotels connected to the platform by a walkway. "It's fine in good weather," he said, "but in bad weather the semis have to pull away from the platform and the bears are transferred to and from the platform by helicopter." It's worth noting that the platform was being completed by these men at the same time as the wells were being drilled, completed and producing oil, with the excess gas being burnt from two huge flare stacks. "I mean," he continued, "800 people all working in a small space – you're going to get a lot of accidents."

I thought, *Well, OK,* but I'd worked in a steelworks for eight years, one of the largest in the world – it was 3 miles long and 1 mile wide – and there were a lot of accidents there, too. I mean, we had 13,000 employees on four shifts working there. So, I decided to get on the bus when it arrived.

I put my bag in the back of the bus and was first on board. I sat in the back seat and a well-dressed silver-haired guy sat next to me. I got chatting to him and asked him what he did on Piper. He was the rig electrician. I told him I'd been talking to the young guy while I waited for the bus and that he'd said there were lots of accidents on Piper. "Well yeah, he's right," he said. "It's a big place with lots of people so yes, there are lots of accidents out there."

Death flashed in front of my eyes and I wondered if maybe I should get off the bus. We were sitting at a red light and I thought, *If I grab my bag and exit through the back door, I could just go back to the railway station and go home.* It was a bit silly really, but this was what was going through my head. But then the lights turned green and off we went down the road and on our way to Dyce.

We arrived at the heliport and I filled out my boarding card. We were given a safety briefing and then got into our survival suits and into the helicopter. This would be the first of many trips but I'd never been in a helicopter before and it was quite exciting. Piper was situated 140 miles off Aberdeen; it was a 45-minute flight, most of it over water.

The pilot announced we would be landing in five

minutes and suddenly I could see in the distance a huge platform sticking out of the water with two big gas flares shooting flames into the sky. Alongside them were two drilling derricks, which I came to know as Rig 34 and Rig 35. We landed on the platform and got out of the helicopter, keeping our heads down as per the briefing. After making our way to the staircase and down the stairs, we were told to wait for our bags to arrive with the roustabout crew, who would get them off the chopper.

They soon arrived, and a man approached me. "I'm Robin, the rig medic," he said. "Come with me. You have to report to the Bawden tool pusher." I soon found out that the tool pusher was the senior manager for Bawden Drilling on that platform. I was rushed down to the office, where I noticed the young guy who told me about all the accidents standing there, which I thought was strange.

The medic said to the tool pusher, "We need someone to go out on tower. We need one of these two guys to go out to work on deck right now, to replace the roustabout that fell off the casing stack on the pipe deck. He's being medevacked onto the chopper now with head injuries."

The tool pusher, an old Canadian guy call Rocky, looked up at us and said, "Well, he's the biggest." He pointed at me. "Send him out there and the other one can go back to the day shift, painting and cleaning." I found out later that the young guy had only been on one tour before this one.

The medic said: "Come with me and I'll show you your locker, where you can store your work gear. Then

I'll show you the four-man room where you will sleep. Then we'll go down to the galley and you can take your lunch."

My eyes lit up as we entered the dining room, for it was huge; it was like being in a fancy restaurant. I mean, there were so many people and *so* much food – soups, steaks, chips, salads, ice cream; whatever you wanted, it was there – and lots of it. I ate a lunch of steak and chips and put my workwear on before arriving on the pipe deck.

I was met there by the roustabout pusher, Peter Ward. It was very noisy on deck and I had a hard time hearing what he had to say because of the whoosh of the two gas flares. I got the gist of what he was on about: get on top of the 13⅜" casing, which was about 6 feet above the deck, and pull on a thick rope to guide the casing into the front of the V-door, so called because it was in the shape of a V. *Well,* I thought *that can't be too difficult.*

The first joint flew past the doorway and banged into the side of the derrick. The roustabout was screaming at me – I couldn't hear him scream, but I knew he was not happy when he threw his hard hat onto the floor. The second joint was excellent, straight in, and the crane driver lowered it down on top of the catwalk. The roughnecks placed an elevator over the box connection and the driller lifted the 40 ft casing joint up into the derrick and lowered the pipe through the hole in the rotary table. There were three holes on the rig floor – the rat hole, used to make up drill collars; the mouse hole, used to make up drill pipe; and the third one, which was in the rotary table, and this was the one they drilled through. While we were running the casing, the crew on the rig floor were helping the casing crew company, PA International, to make up the pin and box casing connections. This would take about eight hours, stopping only after they had run casing to the bottom of the hole, some 5,000 feet below the rotary table.

So, here I was running casing for the first time and at that moment I didn't realise managing oil rig casing around the world would end up being my perversion for the next 40 years.

After my 12-hour shift was over, the roustabout pusher, who turned out to be Australian, came up to me and said, "Not bad, mate, you didn't do a bad job. I think we'll keep you for now and we'll just see how you do. But fuck up and you're on the next chopper!"

I went down to have a shower and a nice meal, followed by a film in the recreation room with the crew before going to sleep. That was my first day in the oilfield.

A Shitty Day at Work

So, I was a roustabout. I completed my first hitch unscathed, having unloaded supply boats, unloaded, loaded and refuelled helicopters, cleaned, painted, ate and slept. The next 14 days off were spent in Aberdeen with my brother and his family. There was a little drinking but hey, I needed to make friends and find out the lay of the land.

Halfway through my next trip on Piper, Peter the roustabout pusher announced that the crew's first job of the day was to unblock the showroom toilets; the bears had blocked them up after they'd had to overnight on the platform because of bad weather. Peter told three guys to pull out the fire hose and take it through to the toilets. Then he told me to turn on the water on his command. A few minutes later, Peter popped his head out of the changing room door and gave me the thumbs up. I opened the valve right up and saw the hosepipe jump with the pressure.

I heard screaming coming from the room. Peter's head came around the door as he shouted: "Turn the bloody thing off!" I turned the valve off and ran to see what the problem was. As I got to the door, the smell was unbearable. The room was metal and mostly tiled, with big sewer hatches on the floor for the human waste to run into – and there was shit and toilet paper covering the ceiling, walls and floor and, yes, the three roustabouts. Peter had been standing far enough away to stay clean. So what had happened? They had stuck the hosepipe down the first toilet and, when I turned the water on, it blew all the shit and paper out of the other five pans!

Peter told two guys to stay back and clean up the mess. A helicopter was coming in to land in 15 minutes and he told me I would be in charge of refuelling it, along with Speedy, the third roustabout, once he had changed his clothes.

This current trip passed pretty quickly and before I knew it, I was back onshore and ready to paint the town red – but this time I went to visit my parents and my brother John and his family in Wales. I arrived back in Aberdeen with a couple of days to spare before returning to Piper Alpha, ready for the next 14 days and whatever this would bring.

Boom Town

I always remember the first time I visited Aberdeen, the Granite City. I drove up from South Wales, some 12 hours from my home in Newport. Towards the end of my journey, I remember driving through Stonehaven, a small village just outside the city. It was late in the day and as I approached the top of the hill, I could see Aberdeen in the distance. It was like looking down on a space age city, all lit up in orange light. I pulled the car over to take in the view. Aberdeen is the last city in Scotland; with the North Sea on one side and the Highlands to the other, it was surrounded by darkness and I hadn't seen anything like it before.

Aberdeen had been a big fishing port but now, with the decline of the industry, most of the fishing boats were being used as safety vessels, floating around the oil platforms on standby just in case of emergencies. Aberdeen is called the Granite City because all the houses and commercial properties are built or surfaced in granite. The city centre is as grey as it comes and, coupled with a grey sky, it can be quite gloomy, but on a sunny day the granite shines and sparkles. Granite was first quarried from Rubislaw Quarry in 1800; it's about a mile or so from Union Street, a straight line of shops, bars, nightclubs and a cinema, and known as the Granite Mile.

The oil industry originally had its headquarters in Great Yarmouth in the east of England, where the first exploration and development drilling started in the 1960s. Now, in the 70s, bigger oil fields had been found off the coast near Aberdeen and the Shetlands: Forties, Piper, Beryl, Brent and Ekofisk, to name a few. There was an influx of people into Aberdeen: mostly Americans, Canadians and Australians with oilfield experience. The price of accommodation doubled overnight. Entrepreneurs invested in building houses and opening pubs, clubs and supermarkets as the onshore service sector went into overdrive.

I was lucky to be able to live with my brother Hadyn and his family during my 14 days onshore, when I was not visiting my mum and dad in Newport. Hadyn lived in Fountainhall Road in the west end of Aberdeen, next to Grampian Television Studios and just around the corner from the Dutch Mill Hotel. This was one of my regular watering holes, where I would meet up with my new friends, mostly oilfield guys from New Zealand and Australia. I also had a few good Aberdonion friends. In those days, Scotland's pubs used to close at 10 pm and if they weren't hotels, they were also closed on Sundays. So, at 10 pm, you would hear someone call: "Last orders, please!" and you'd find out where the party was that night. The parties would be at someone's house or flat and everyone was invited – you didn't need to know the person, just bring a six-pack of beer with you. Most parties ended around 2 or 3 am but I did find myself waking up once or twice at some stranger's house at midday.

Not a lot of money was being saved at this time. Aberdeen was awash with good-looking local girls; in all my time running around the town, I never met a hooker. Some of the most attractive girls would ask you straight away what your job was. They were mostly looking for high earners like saturation divers, who spent two or three months offshore at a time. Saturation diving was a dangerous job and paid big money and when they came to town, the divers went wild, throwing their money around as if there was no tomorrow. If a girl's first question to me was, "What's your job?" I would tell her I was a milkman, just to see if she would walk away. Then I'd tell her I was a roustabout. I had a few girlfriends but found it difficult to hold onto them after being badly burned by my first wife, who I dated for six years. Our marriage only lasted 12 months before she ran off with a fellow school teacher.

There is one Aberdeen party that has stuck in my mind all these years. We'd arrived at the train station having just finished 14 days offshore on the Piper Alpha, and my Aberdonion mate Speedy asked me if I wanted to go to a party. When I asked him when it was, he said, "Now!" When I pointed out it was 2.30 in the afternoon he said, "Yes, that's right. Let's go."

We arrived at a small flat in Torry, near the docks. I could hear the music blaring out – the Bee Gees' *Saturday Night Fever*. Once inside, peering through the thick cigarette smoke, I could see the place was packed with people dancing and drinking. Speedy handed me a beer and he jumped right into the dancing.

I started chatting to a few people. There was one guy having a whale of a time on the dance floor. He came over to get a beer and introduced himself as Doug. "Boy,"

I said, "you're having a good time!"

"Yes!" he said, with a big smile on his face. "I was up in court this morning for drink driving."

"What did you get?" I asked, thinking he would say a 12-month ban and a big fine.

"A 25-year ban!"

Twenty-five years? I checked I'd heard him right and he said yes. "So why are you so happy?" I asked.

"Well," he said, "this was the third time the police caught me this year and my solicitor told me I was looking at a jail sentence. So I am pleased that I am not down the road, locked up in Craiginches!"

Climbing the Ladder

I was into my fourth trip offshore and had just been told by the tool pusher that I had been promoted to roughneck on Rig 35. I had been relieving the guys on the rig floor who were running drill pipes in or out of the hole, so they could take their meals and at 'smoke-o time'. These were taken twice a shift in a container on the pipe deck. Here, the guys could have a smoke and there was food available 24/7: sandwiches, cakes, coffee, tea and soft drinks. My favourite was chocolate éclairs with fresh cream.

Now, I thought I was pretty fit and could handle anything thrown at me; I mean, I was only 25. But on my first day as a roughneck we pulled out of the hole 15,000 feet of drill pipe, setting the heavy rotary hand slips around the drill pipe every few minutes, breaking out the connection and pulling out the slips again and again for 12 hours. By the end of the shift, I was fucked. I even dreamed I was pulling slips in my sleep and woke up feeling like a train had hit me. Before long, I was working the derrick, relieving the derrick man for his breaks. I had no problem working 90 feet from the rig floor on the monkey board and I did this for a few more trips. Then we were told that Rig 35 was to be decommissioned and we were taken off Piper Alpha; only Rig 34 would stay to compete the drilling.

During my first 18 months in the oil industry, I learned a lot about drilling oil wells and had seen many oil service crews play their part at different periods during the drilling process. Drilling a well is like building a house: there are lots of people involved, such as the land owner (oil company), builder (drilling company), tradesmen, electrician, plumber, carpenter, roofer (wire-line, casing crews, cementation companies, mud companies, casing and tubing supply companies) and so on.

I didn't know then that, eleven years later, on 6th July 1988, I would turn on my TV to see a news flash showing the devastating explosions on Piper Alpha. Safety lapses aboard the platform resulted in a series of explosions, which, in under three hours, claimed the lives of 165 out of the 226 men on board. With only 61 survivors and approximately $3.4 billion total insured damages, the Piper Alpha disaster remains one of the worst such events in the history of the oil and gas sector.

Derrickman, Montrose Alpha

Bawden told me they would find me a new position on one of their other rigs but I would probably have to stay onshore for a month or two. *Not bad*, I thought, but four days into my fourteen days off I was told to report to the railway station. I had been made up to derrickman on the AMOCO platform Montrose Alpha. Arriving on board Montrose Alpha, the first thing that struck me was that it was a much smaller platform than Piper: it had only one gas flare and could only accommodate 96 personnel.

I was told by the Bawden Tool Pusher that there were two derrickmen on each tower due to running oil-based mud into the hole because of some stuck pipe problems. I had worked with oil-based mud on Piper; this mud was very expensive to use compared with the much cheaper water-based bentonite mud. Oil-based mud is a mixture of chemicals, diesel, sulphur and other nasty shit; it would burn your skin if you came into contact with it. I was happy when the tool pusher told me I would be running the derrick and the other derrickmen would be in the mud pit look after the mud.

My first hitch went off without a problem. The job was the same whichever derrick you were working on: get the pipe in/out of the hole as fast as you can without dropping a stand. (A stand is made up of three joints about 30 feet long, making a stand 90 feet in height. The bottom assembly is made up of the drill bit, stabilizer collars and heavyweight drill pipe.)

Midway through my second trip, we had an incident on the rig floor. I was working the night shift and we were drilling, so I only had to be in the derrick once we needed to make up a 90-foot stand. I was talking to the driller when all of a sudden, the rig floor lit up in a bright blue flash and there was a deafening thunder clap. We looked at each other and then at the crew standing nearby – our hair was sticking straight out of the sides of our safety helmets and the hair on our bodies was standing on end too! But then came the call: "Fire, fire, fire!" The mud shaker had been hit by lightning and was on fire. We ran for the powder fire extinguishers and it took us a good five minutes to get it under control.

The AMACO company man and the Bawden tool pusher were out of their beds and onto the rig floor in a flash, looking white-faced as they shouted: "What the fuck happened?" Once the fire was out, we spent the rest of the shift cleaning up the mess and thankful that we had managed to get the fire under control. At that point, I reflected that my oilfield career may have been a very short one. We were drilling for the rest of the hitch and I was glad to see Aberdeen from the helicopter window and meet up with my friends to swap stories over a pint of beer.

I arrived back aboard Montrose to see the roustabouts and drill crew were running production tubing in the hole. This is one of the jobs for which the oil company would call out a casing crew. They would supply the air-operated elevator and spider, tubing tong and power unit, plus a computer to monitor the correct make-up torque on each pin and box connection when they were made up. The company used on Piper Alpha was PA International but these guys worked for Weatherford Lamb. When Weatherford were running or pulling casing or tubing, there was very little for me to do, other than maintenance on the derrick, but part of my job was to relieve the Weatherford stabber for meals and smoke-o breaks. In turn, the stabber relieved the tong operator and the operator relieved the computer technician. The stabber's job was to stand on a narrow stabbing board that was hanging from the side of the derrick, 40 feet up from the rig floor. The board was air operated and could travel up and down five feet as the pipe was never the same length and could alter by up to one or two feet in length. I had experience of stabbing pipes on Piper Alpha; the Montrose wells were not as deep as Piper's, only around 11,000 feet. The job was completed without incident and the Weatherford crew ran the string into the hole in under 24 hours.

I was impressed and a little jealous that they only stayed on board for three days before going back to town. I sat next to one of the Weatherford guys in the galley and he said they were hiring and I should drop by their office in Dyce and ask to see the personnel manager. He also told me he had just returned from a job in Brazil…

Now, I always wanted a job that would take me around the world so, after completing my 14 days offshore, I drove out to Weatherford's base in Dyce and picked up their employment questionnaire. On my way home I got it photocopied, just in case I made a mistake while I was filling it out. I worked on it for a couple of hours, returned the paperwork the next morning and was told I'd got the job as a trainee technician.

Weatherford, UK: New Job, New Wife

After leaving Bawden Drilling – which, I must say, was a good company to work for – I had to start thinking about moving higher up the ladder. However, the responsibility of being a driller or tool pusher, with all the paperwork, form filling and periodic training that came with the job, was frightening. The thought of it took me back to school, the place I hated throughout my childhood because of my dyslexia. I mean, I could do it; given the time and with no one looking over my shoulder, my reading and writing had improved, but my spelling was atrocious. When I first look at a page of a book, I can't formulate the words. They all seem to be moving about. It's like your brain wants you to speed-read but your eyes can't focus. I have to read the page two or three times to make sense of it.

I was looking for something different that would both pay well and take me around the world with as little paperwork as possible! Working on a platform for 14 days and having 14 days off wasn't a bad life but it was like turning up to the same factory and workmates every month. Now I had the opportunity to travel – but I would have to start again at the bottom.

The weekend before starting with Weatherford, I was having a drink at the Dutch Mill and across the room I recognised the Weatherford receptionist, Elaine. She was standing with a girlfriend who stood out from the crowd because she was dressed in a dark green velvet trouser suit. I went up to Elaine to say hi and was introduced to Ellie Watt; Ellie also worked for Weatherford and was the PA to Eddie Colden, the UK regional manager. Ellie and I hit it off from the get-go and were married nine months later at Aberdeen University chapel. Another white wedding. But not before Ellie had to resign because of Weatherford's employment contract, which stated that no married couple could work together. She started a new job with Schlumberger as PA to the UK manager, based in their main office off Union Street.

We bought a small third-floor flat in Watson Street, which overlooked the main entrance to Victoria Park. Before moving in, we refurbished the whole apartment; eighteen months later, we sold it and started to move up the housing ladder, each time making a very good profit on the sale. We learned it was always important to purchase in a good location – plus the number of new people moving into Aberdeen kept escalating the housing prices.

I thought I would be sent offshore as soon as I started but instead, I spent the first month in a workshop. We were given training on power tongs, power units and elevators, but most of the training was practical rather than theory, and most of the time I was putting hinged centralizers together. These came in all the casing sizes: 7", 7⅝", 9⅝", 13⅜", 18⅝" and 20". Centralizers are placed around the box connection or sometime in the middle of the casing joint prior to running down a hole; they are fastened with nails run through both hinges and bent over to keep them on the pipe. Once the casing string is sitting just off the bottom of the hole, the cementing company takes over, pumping cement down through the inside of the casing and out of the cement shoe, filling the outside of the casing between the casing and annulus of the well. The is done to prevent gas from coming up through the gap between the casing and annulus but, for a good cement job, the casing has to have good centralization to prevent it from lying on the wall of the annulus. A bad cement job can lead to a blowout, creating the possibility of loss of life and destruction of the rig should the escaping gas or oil catch fire. At this time, I didn't think centralizers and float equipment would play such a big part in my 40 years in the oilfield.

My first job offshore as a trainee was running 8,000 feet of 9⅝" casing and you won't believe which platform it was for… Yes, the Montrose Alpha. AMOCO always called the crew out at the last minute so on arrival we just had time to check the equipment before we started the job. As I walked onto the rig floor, I heard the crew clapping their hands and the driller shout out: "So you couldn't stay away!" Bollocks! It was my old Bawden crew and I knew they wouldn't make this job easy for me.

The job started and the stabber said: "Come with me up to the stabbing board. I'll do the first couple of joints and then it will be your turn." I had stabbed on this board before, relieving casing stabbers when I was the derrick man here. Little did I know but this time I would be left up on the board for the remainder of the job. Neither the Weatherford stabber nor the Bawden derrick man came to relieve me, they sent coffee and sandwiches sent up attached to the side of the elevator. However, the job went well; no crossed joints needed to be backed out and it took just 10 hours. Then it was back to town the next day and a night out with my buddies. *This is not a bad life,* I was thinking.

Back in the yard the next day, Ted Leslie, the service supervisor told me I needed to complete two training jobs before making grade one technician; then I would start being paid an offshore bonus and a second bonus payment if I was sent out as a stabber. Ted told me the Shell Stadrill Rig was my next job. I had friends who were working on semi-subs, so I knew a little about them. However, I had never worked on a semi-submersible before as I had only been on production platforms, so this was to be a new adventure for me.

This job was running 13⅜″ casing string about 5,000 feet long. I got the idea I would be back in three days at the most, but we were 12 days aboard the rig before we even started to run the job. Alan the stabber told me I would be working with him stabbing the pipe. We helped set up the power unit and power tong before climbing 40 feet up the derrick to the stabbing board. I hadn't seen a board like this one before – well, there was no board, just a flap of metal grating measuring about three feet long by two feet wide, with a rope to let it out and pull it back. It was situated behind the tracks that were carrying the rotary blocks; normally the board would be situated to the side of the blocks. Working on this board was hairy as you stood with the derrick at your back and the blocks passing very, very close to the front of you. Alan said: "You'll be OK. Just don't forget to pull the flap back after you have stabbed the casing or the blocks will rip the fucking grating off and kill someone on the rig floor."

The job started and Alan did the first three joints before saying, "It's your turn. I will keep an eye on you to make sure you get the idea." The bastard didn't tell me he would be keeping his eye on me from the rig floor 40 feet below me; in fact, I didn't see him again until the end of the job! It started off OK, although I did cross two joints and the tong operator had to back them out and rerun them. I remembered to pull up the flap: the driller was very fast and the blocks would pass me at some speed; you had to push yourself back against the derrick for them to miss you. It was the middle of the job, I had just stabbed a joint and then there was a short delay when, all of a sudden, the derrick started to shake and hammers and shackles fell off the monkey board some 50 feet above my head, hitting the metal stanchions of the derrick on their way down and landing a further 40 feet below me on the rig floor. Then these huge chain links started to appear from both sides of the blocks. Finally, the penny dropped: the weather had picked up and the waves were getting bigger. The driller was having to compensate with the casing string to be able to continue running it down the hole.

I was always fascinated on a semi, looking at the casing string from the rig floor. It always looked like the pipe was moving up and down and you were standing still but of course you were going up and down and the pipe was standing still. It's a little like being in a train carriage: the train next to you pulls away out of the station and you think you're moving.

After these two training jobs, I was ready to see the world and get paid for it.

My first few years with Weatherford were spent working in the North Sea, mainly on platforms like Brent and Beryl. The Brent field was made up of four platforms: the first platform installed was the concrete-legged Brent Bravo, followed by Brent Delta, Brent Charlie and steel-jacketed Brent Alpha. Weatherford had the contract for the four platforms, but the problem with working on the Brent field was that Shell were always short of accommodation. I mean, this was a huge development and not only did the platform have accommodation but there were at least four or five semis that had been converted to hotels (flotels) to house the bears (construction workers) that were working on the four platforms – literally hundreds of guys moving back and forth every twelve hours. The flotels were attached by a walkway from the semi to the platform, but in bad weather they would have to pull away for safety reasons and the bears would be shuttled back and forth by helicopter. It was said that at one time there were more landings and take offs per day than at Heathrow Airport in London. No end of times we would land on the platform, only to be told they were not ready for us to start work and we would have to sleep in a sleeping bag on the floor of the library, where you couldn't get any rest because people were coming and going in and out of the room all night, light on, light off. Also, the Shell jobs seemed to take longer than those with other oil companies and once they had you in the field, they liked to keep you as long as they could, before sending you back to Aberdeen.

At this time, I was spending up to twenty-eight days offshore per month. The money was good, but it wasn't the type of job that gave you a decent home life, and marriages did suffer. So I wasn't doing as much socialising, but I was starting to save a little money.

I was sent out to most of the jobs as a stabber and I gained further experience by relieving the power tong operator on breaks when we were running large OD casing and there were only the two of us in the crew. When it came to tubing completions, the depth of the completion would determine the crew size. Running 4½" tubing, say, 12,000 feet, the crew would be made up of a JAM tech (Joint Analyse Make-up technician), a tong operator and a stabber, and maybe a combination man who could run all the equipment. These jobs could take up to 24-36 hours non-stop. I once had a job running 7" Atlas Bradford casing on the Brent Alpha that lasted in excess of 60 hours; there was a leak in the string, found when the Shell engineers ran a pressure test. We ran and pulled and pressure-tested the string to try and find out where the leak was coming from. On this job we didn't have a combination man; there were only three of us in the crew. JAM techs won't normally stab pipe so we depended on the derrick man to let the stabber go and eat, and the stabber let me eat. The JAM tech in this case had to eat his food on the rig floor and took a shit in between pressure tests. To make things even worse, the Brent field was fogged in; we had crews on the other three platforms but the choppers couldn't fly.

I remember falling asleep leaning against the drawworks in between making or breaking the pipe out. By now, the rig crew were helping by putting the tong on the pipe and then waking me up from my slumber. I had to look underneath the power tong each time to see if I was making or breaking the pipe out: if I could see threads then I was making it up and you'd better know what gear the tong was in; trying to break out pipe in high gear was a no no, as the tong would fly back at you like a bullet, whipping anyone standing in its path and only stopping when its safety sling stopped its motion. At last they found the problem. The engineers ran a green dye in the completion fluid and could see it seeping through a pin end thread, which had a crack. We laid this joint out on the pipe deck, picked a new 7" casing joint and ran the string back into the hole and the string tested OK. By now, the fog had lifted and I could see from the rig V-door Weatherford technicians coming off the choppers to help us. I felt like crying.

I bet you're thinking: "Les, you must have slept for 24 hours after that." Yes and no. I just could not go to sleep. After hours of lying there, I started counting sheep – as you do if you come from Wales – and I woke up 24 hours later.

I would see other senior technicians being sent off to run jobs in other countries. This is what I wanted to do, but it wouldn't happen until I had managed to get to grade three, some 18 months later. Until then, the North Sea jobs kept coming.

While I was working on Brent Alpha, I was told by the

Shell rep that I was needed for a job on Brent Charlie. I packed my bag and made my way to the departure room to wait for the chopper. I was led out to the helideck and there stood a bright red Robinson R-22 Beta II, 2-seater helicopter. I had never been in one of these before. I sat next to the pilot and he handed me a set of earphones and a microphone. The chopper came up off the helideck by about three feet. It moved to the outer side of the deck – most helidecks are about 160 feet above sea level – and we just dropped off the edge towards the sea at a fast rate of knots. I nearly shit myself! I thought I was going to die. The pilot laughed and said: "Don't worry, I have to do that so we can pick up enough speed to get height enough to be able to land on Brent Charlie." The field was a little foggy. We had been in the air for only a couple of minutes and I couldn't see Charlie. Then the pilot pointed at the fuel gauge, which read empty. I was beginning to think the trip was doomed. We hit an air pocket and dropped 20 feet. My heart was in my mouth. The pilot looked at me and turned a switch on the dashboard – the gauge suddenly read full and we landed on Charlie with no further problems.

I really didn't like working in the North Sea. It always seemed to be wet and windy and, working on the stabbing board, there were no metal wind walls to protect you; they stopped about 15 feet above the rig floor, and the next wind walls were a further 75 feet up, around the monkey board where the derrickmen stood. We stabbers, 40 feet above the rig floor, were out there in the elements. You could see the rain coming towards you minutes before it arrived. One time, I was on the stabbing board and the snow was coming at me horizontally; I was covered in snow from head to toe. And you were lucky if anyone came to relieve you and let you go to the bathroom and eat. One time, I was so cold that when the derrick man came up to let me go for food, I couldn't move my fingers and had to be taken down to the rig floor on a man-riding tugger. Once I was in the changing room, I ran hot water over my hands. We've all had pins and needles when we've been out too long in the cold, but this was close to frostbite.

I don't remember doing a job that didn't have a problem that needed resolving. We would run equipment for 30" conductor all the way down to 2⅜" tubing and you had to keep this equipment running. Every minute lost to down time would cost the oil company thousands of dollars and this would make the company man very pissed off – and you know what they say: "Shit rolls downhill." So NO PRESSURE… It was all about getting the pipe in the hole as fast as possible – and that's when accidents can happen.

I remember running a 2⅜" tubing string using a very small hydraulic power tong called a Hillman Kelly 500. When I was relieved by the stabber, I asked him if he had run a Hillman Kelly before and he said no. So I told him, "When you operate this tong, you treat it like a lady, nice and gentle, and with respect – or it will slap you right in the face!" The tong was very small to work with: pulling it on and off the pipe was easy but if you pushed the throttle handle in too fast, it would grab the pipe so fast the power unit would go into overdrive and the tong would come back at you like a bullet – and yes, this is exactly what happened. He was catapulted across the rig floor and landed up against a rack of drill pipes.

Fortunately, he was OK, just badly bruised and shaken. The driller walked over to me and said: "We'll have some sandwiches sent up from the galley. And from now on, you are the only one allowed to run that tong."

In the industry, the Hillman Kelly is known as 'the Humane Killer' – and now you know why.

Weatherford, Italy

My next job was in Italy. At the time, Weatherford was the biggest TRS (Tubular Running Service) in the world and had around 40 bases globally. Italy had more gas wells than oil wells and there were working rigs both on and offshore; they had a lot of work requiring extra TRS technicians. Weatherford Ravenna was located between San Marino and Bologna in the northern Italian province of Emilia Romagna. The manager for Italy was called Don Caponigro and he walked around with his overcoat wrapped over his shoulders; he looked like he was connected, if you know what I mean.

I arrived at the base to find three other guys from the UK: one from the Great Yarmouth base and two from Aberdeen. They were in the yard tossing pennies at a wall: the nearest penny to the wall would win and picked up the money. *Guys, you're in Italy!* I thought. *There must be something better to do!* The next day, I was the only one left at the base as the others had all gone on jobs. After being given a week's daily food allowance by Spalatcy, the service supervisor, I went back to the Hotel Ravenna, changed and went sightseeing. There are a number of beautifully preserved historical sites in Ravenna, including buildings with delicate early Christian mosaics. For example, the extraordinary basilica is a marvellous example of early Christian Byzantine art and architecture, and whilst the outside may appear a little drab, the interior is bursting with dazzling mosaics. Ravenna is famous for its 5th and 6th century mosaics, as well as new offerings by local artists, and I noticed that several of the street signs had been created by local mosaicists. After visiting some sights, I had lunch at Piazza del Popolo, a lovely little square where you can indulge in an aperitif and a spot of people-watching. Who doesn't love a languid late afternoon drink whilst casting one's eye over a well-dressed Italian crowd? I was on my own and soaking in the hot sun.

The next day I was off on a job with a young Italian technician, Marco, who turned up in a very small Fiat 500. We were off to Parma, the university city famous for Parmesan cheese and Parma ham. We took the autostrada towards Milan and had been travelling for a while when all of a sudden, the traffic slowed down because of a major road accident. There was a truck on its side that had come over from the other carriageway, hitting four cars and badly damaging them. There were bodies and shoes littering the road, men's and women's. I hadn't seen or have since seen such carnage. As we passed, the police were busy covering the bodies with coats. Marco picked up speed and thrashed the little engine but I told him to slow down as I would like to live. This experience had really upset me.

We finally exited the autostrada and arrived just outside the town of Parmigiano Reggiano – and there stood the biggest land rig I had ever seen. This rig had double BOPs – Blowout Preventers, which control the well pressure and are closed around the pipe if there are any well problems; they can also cut through the pipe to totally seal the well. The rig floor was 50 feet off the ground and there was a lift to take you up. We reported to a company man who worked for the Italian oil giant Agip (Saipem owned the rig) and he asked us to check out our equipment: power unit and power tong, dressed for running 3½" Hydril PH6 tubing. This tubing would be used as a kill string. In some cases, especially when suspension or temporary well abandonment is requested, it can be useful for operational and safety reasons to run in the hole a killing string. This is usually made up of tubing and ensures that when the well is re-entered, pressure control and circulation is possible down to the defined depth. After checking our equipment, we powered up the unit, hooked up the hoses and rotated the 3½" tong jaws. I could see straight away we had a problem. The base had only sent one set of hydraulic hoses and they were too short to go from the ground up to the drill floor. So, in the lift, up to the V-door and across the drill floor I went to talk to the driller. He didn't speak English, and Marco was nowhere to be seen. The driller called the tool pusher, who came to the floor. His English was OK, so I told him the problem and it was decided to place the power unit on the roof of the drawworks. This would never have been allowed in the North Sea as it would put the power unit too close to the rotary table that we would be running the tubing through. The problem is that if there was any escaping gas from the well, the power unit's hot exhaust pipe could ignite the gas, resulting in an explosion and causing the well to blow out uncontrollably into a towering inferno. This was the beginning of me finding out that safety was not the number one concern here.

Later that night, we started to run the tubing back in the hole using the rig's elevators and slips. The tubing was already in stands, three joints making a stand of 90 feet. The derrickman was on the monkey board latching the elevators around the pipe, so there was no need for a stabber. Once we'd rigged up the equipment, Marco said he would take the first six hours and I should go to bed. Back at ground level, I could feel the vibrations from the Hough rig pumps coming up through my whole body. There was no accommodation on site, because the drill crews didn't work 12-hour shifts; they worked 8-hours shifts and these guys all had rooms in town. So I slept on the floor of the coffee shack in my coveralls. It was very cold and I woke up stiff as a board, grabbed a coffee and made my way to the rig floor.

As soon as I got there, Marco told me they were changing crews and going for breakfast. Everyone was getting on to the bus. I decided I needed shut down our power unit as we would not be on site if there was a problem. I could hear the company man shouting up at me not to bother shutting down the unit and to get on the bus, but I shut down the unit anyway. I sat next to the company man during breakfast and asked him if the motorman had been left on the rig as they were still circulating the hole. "No," he said, "that's him at the end of the table." So no one was at the rig... I was gobsmacked.

Back on the rig floor, everything seemed OK. I started the power unit and began making up pipe. I thought back to earlier in the day: I had taken a walk across the road to the local cemetery where I walked through an archway into a courtyard with a water fountain in the middle. The four inner walls were where the dead were entombed. Each headstone had a name, dates of birth and death, and a picture of the person. It was very interesting to see how other cultures dealt with their dead. Looking across from the rig floor, I could see the lanterns swinging back and forth outside the cemetery and as I felt the vibrations coming from the rig pumps, I wondered if the bodies in the walls were vibrating in their coffins. I think the autostrada victims were still playing on my mind.

The rest of the job continued without any problems and I arrived back in Ravenna to be told I would be returning to Aberdeen the next day. But I hadn't been home a week before I was told to go back to Ravenna! Back at the base, Spalatcy told me I would be going offshore the next day and that someone would pick me up from the hotel at 7 am; I would be taking a boat from Pescara to the Agip platform Emilia.

This time, I would be working with Javani. He drove down through Ravenna and we stopped for breakfast at a coffee bar. The Italians always had an espresso, single shot, in a small cup, with a shot of something like Sambuca. Javani finished his breakfast – bread, butter, jam and croissants – and then we were off on a short drive down the coast. We arrived at the dock in Pescara and boarded a hydroplane workboat. You could see the platform from the dock and the trip there didn't take very long. The boat slowed down and reversed slowly until it touched the platform cellar deck walkway. The chain railing was unlatched and we were told to jump off onto the walkway when the boat was level with it. The sea that day was pretty calm but you had to time the jump right.

We climbed the stairs from the cellar deck to the pipe deck and went to see the company man to introduce ourselves. Then we went out to the pipe deck to check our equipment. We were told later that they were having some hole problems and they would let us know when they were ready for us. We would be running a 2⅜" kill string and again the tubing was in stands in the derrick, so no stabber was required. I couldn't believe I was running another kill string – if this carried on, I would become known as The Kill String Man – but I was glad I was on an offshore platform as at least I would get a bed and decent food from the galley. Another bonus: alcohol is not allowed on oil rigs or oilfields anywhere in the world except Italy! On each table, there were two jugs: a white jug containing white wine and a brown jug with red wine. I thought I had died and gone to heaven! And the best thing was when they were empty, you put the jug on your head and whatever colour it was, the waiter would bring you a replacement. I never saw anyone drunk on the rig, so I guess it wasn't a problem.

Two days later, we started the job. After rigging up, I said to Javani that I would take the first shift of six hours and he left the rig floor to me. There had been no room on the pipe deck to let us inspect or even see the power tong, only the power unit, and Javani told me he had checked them both back at base and they were both running OK. I looked at the tubing tong and at first thought it was a Hillman Kelly 500c but, on closer inspection, it said Hillman Kelly on the tong but it wasn't a 500c; it was a tong I had never seen before. Next thing I knew, the rig crew were putting the tong on the pipe – I could see it had a throttle handle and gear changer, but the throttle only moved forward and to release the jaws, you pumped the throttle and they released their grip. *So how do you back out a joint?* I thought. I just had to hope the crew would know what to do if I had a crossed thread connection – and bloody hell, the sixth make up the pin was crossed in the box connection. This meant I had to back it out. I looked at the crew and they looked at me. I had noticed a metal bar poking out from the back of the tong, the end bent into an L-shape. I thought, *Fuck it,* and I pulled the pin towards me. All of a sudden, the tong flipped upside down! I pushed the throttle handle inward, the rotor went into reverse and I backed out the joint. The look on the faces of the crew was one of fascination – they hadn't seen this before. The tong was top heavy and, the motor and gearbox now being upside down, it took three of us to turn it back up and push the pin back in. Then we carried on making up pipe, luckily with no more crossed joints. Javani replaced me six hours later and he finished the job.

The next morning, we were told to make our way down to the cellar deck to board the hydroplane workboat back to Pescara. Waiting for the boat was the drill crew I had worked with. The boat arrived and one man got off, but it was windy, the waves were a little higher than the day we arrived and the captain was having problems keeping the boat still against the landing dock. The boat crew told us to throw our bags onto the boat, which then had to pull away as the front of the boat was pushed up high onto the cellar deck. The boat came in again and its crew stood by to help us aboard. The driller was at the front of the line. He stepped down onto a ledge about 6" lower than the cellar deck and as he did, the boat veered up again and crushed his foot. I will always remember his screams... There was blood everywhere, a crushed shoe – and what was left of his right foot landed in front of me.

The captain pulled the boat away from the landing dock and his crew mates were able to pull him onto the cellar deck so he didn't fall into the sea. I looked down at where his foot should be but all that was left was an ankle. The captain again brought the hydroplane back to the platform but this time it was full throttle: you could hear the engines roaring as an Italian voice came over the boat radio. The two crew members and the driller boarded the boat, the engines went into reverse and it pulled away about 50 feet from the platform. Then the personnel basket was lowered from the pipe deck by the platform crane. The basket landed on the back of the boat and the driller was loaded into it. Pescara was only two miles away and before we knew it, there was a helicopter landing on board the helideck to take the driller to hospital.

Now it was my turn to board the boat, along with the remaining personnel. The boat came in and again the captain pushed it hard against the landing. The catwalk shuddered as I jumped aboard, helped by the deck crew. I made sure I didn't put my foot down on the lower ledge. Javani told me later that the driller had to have what was left of his leg amputated below the knee, but he was doing OK.

Later that night, I went out for dinner at a fancy four-star hotel. After my main course, the waiter arrived with a sweet trolley full of desserts. Straight away my eyes were fixated on the fresh cream chocolate gateau, so I asked for a piece. The waiter burst out laughing. "What are you laughing about?" I said.

"Gatto!" he said, still laughing. "You just ordered cat!"

"Cat?" I said.

"Yes!"

"Well, what do you call it then?" I asked him.

"Cake, of course!"

This gave me something to smile about after a bad day.

The next day I was off again, with a crew of five Italian technicians. We arrived in Pescara to catch a chopper to a jackup rig, but first the crew said we should eat in Pescara as by the time we reached the rig we would have just missed lunch. They said Pescara was known for its very good fish restaurants and they weren't wrong.

The chopper ride to the jackup took about 30 minutes and on arrival, as usual, we checked in with the company man and then checked the equipment. This time we were running a dual tubing string of 2⅜" EUE box and pin connections. I had never run a dual completion before; there's not a lot of them run in the North Sea. A dual string is run in the hole with a special elevator and spiders normally manufactured by Barco, using Hillman 500c (Killer) power tongs. The Hillman is used because the tongs are small enough to get around the tubing and grip each pipe for make-up prior to being lowered into the single wellbore, which enables production from two segregated zones, in this case gas. In most cases, two tubing strings will be used to provide the necessary level of control and safety for the fluids from both zones. However, in some simple dual completions, a second or upper zone is produced further up the tubing; they are referred to as the long string and the short string. I found out that running dual completion strings was very slow and that's why we had two crews aboard; even then, the job took three days to complete.

After packing the equipment away and showering, I went to the galley for dinner. The rig crew were from Yugoslavia and they were just sitting down to eat when, on Yugoslavian television, news came that President Tito had died. The whole room exploded with men standing up, shouting and screaming. They were very upset and I didn't understand why. I thought the guy was a dictator and not liked by the Yugoslavs. Looking back, I can see that these guys must have known that, without his leadership, the whole country would eventually break up. Tito's death was followed by a decade of attempts to hold the multi-ethnic country together; the ethnic war would eventually be the bloodiest war in Europe since World War II.

Returning to Ravenna, I met two guys from Aberdeen, Doug and Peter, who I had worked with on several jobs in the North Sea. They had been told they were on standby for a job that should come up in three days; Spalatcy told me that my next job wouldn't be called in for two days. So the three of us decided to take a day trip to San Marino. Surrounded by Italy, landlocked San Marino is one of the smallest countries and oldest republics in the world. The first constitution is from 1263; it is an echo from an era when city-states proliferated across Europe. The entire area of San Marino is only 61km^2 yet there are more than 30,000 inhabitants. What we were interested in was that it was noted for having very cheap wine, beer and spirits. We arrived and had lunch at a very nice restaurant and yes, we did try a few drinks – I say we, but I was the designated driver and the hire car was on my credit card, so not a lot of drinking for me. I did, however, purchase a couple of bottles of wine and some Scottish malt for back at the hotel and at home.

I had never seen Peter drink alcohol before yet he purchased a huge carafe of white wine, the outside covered in string and, as I drove us back to the hotel, I could see him in the rear-view mirror drinking from it. All of a sudden, Peter shouted that he needed a piss. Doug told him we'd be back at the hotel soon. Now, by the sound of Peter's voice I could tell he had drunk a bit too much wine. "Stop the car, stop the car or I will pee myself!" he shouted. I stopped the car just outside a farm gate. Peter got out of the car, still holding the huge carafe by one of its handles, and rushed into the farmyard, where he stopped near a shed. He undid his fly, walked forward and WHAM! A garden rake that was pointing out towards his foot flicked up and hit him straight between the eyes. We were speechless. He stepped backward, stepped forwards and again the rake hit him between the eyes – except this time he did a 90-degree turn to the right and finished his pee. Peter got back in the car, still holding his carafe, with a line of blue bruising down his forehead. Doug and I were curled up laughing in the front seats.

I dropped the two of them off at the hotel and returned the car. As I walked back through the hotel door, I could hear the manager shouting at Doug: "You can clean your friend's mess up!" Peter had been walking up the polished granite stairs, and just before he reached the top he slipped and let go of the carafe to stop his fall. It had smashed all over the staircase and there was glass and wine everywhere.

At breakfast the next morning, I asked Peter how he got the bruise between his eyes. "I don't know," he said, and he never believed our story.

I walked over to the base and Spalatcy told me that the rig had called and they needed me to go that afternoon. I was going back to the offshore platform Emilia, where the driller had lost his foot in the boat accident. I was to pull out a kill string in stands; this would be a quick job and only needed one technician. I jumped into one of the company cars, drove to Pescara and took a chopper out to the rig. No boat this time! The job started around 10 in the morning and should only take around five hours to finish but, with no other technicians on board to let me go for lunch, I was told food and drink would be sent up to the rig floor for me.

The job was going OK, with plenty of stands of tubing

racked back in the derrick. I could see a roustabout carrying a cardboard box up to the rig floor. It was my lunch and he put it down on the step in front of the drawworks. I finished backing out the joint and walked over to see what they had sent me. There was a big plate of sandwiches and some cakes, but nothing to drink. I asked the driller if someone could get me a drink of something. The next thing I knew, a bottle of beer was in the box. I mean, BEER! I had never seen anyone drink alcohol on a rig floor; like smoking, it was forbidden. But hey, this was Italy. So I ate my sandwiches and finished the small bottle of beer in between breaking out the tubing connection. I looked down at the box and another beer had arrived. Now I did start to think about safety – after all, I was using the Hillman killer to break out the connections – but it was hot and I was thirsty, so I drank it. During the next break, I stopped and told the very nice roughneck that I could not drink any more beer – I mean, I could, but not without the chance of hurting someone or doing something stupid with the power tong. I knew I would never drink alcohol on a rig floor again but what I didn't realise was that this would be my last job in Italy.

I loved Italy and its people and I gained a lot of experience in the jobs I ran, but I haven't been back in over 42 years. There was so much more left to see and explore in the world.

Abidjan, Ivory Coast, West Africa

I returned back to base in Aberdeen after four weeks in Italy. I'd been away from Aberdeen for 80 per cent of the previous six months, and Ellie wasn't happy. I talked to Bill Burnett, my base manager, and explained that I needed some time at home. Bill said he understood and that he would put me on some training courses at the base. In particular, I needed to get my Robert Gordon Institute of Technology (RGIT) 3-day offshore survival training certificate, as it was now mandatory for all offshore workers and the training needed to be renewed every two years. This training gave you the basics in first aid, fire-fighting, underwater helicopter escape and lifeboat survival.

So, I had a break of 14 days and bang, I was sent away to help organise a new Weatherford base in Abidjan in the Ivory Coast, West Africa. The Ivory Coast got its independence from France in 1960 and was French speaking. It was well known for its religious and ethnic harmony, as well as its well-developed economy – and now its new oil fields.

The first day there, I met the Dutch service supervisor, Burt Cook. He told me to come with him to register a new pickup truck. I thought this was a good time to take a look around Abidjan. Burt was waiting for his international driving licence to arrive from Holland but I already had one, so I was driving. We had to stop at a red traffic light. There were three other cars in front of us, and for some reason the second car ran into the back of the first car. The two drivers were out of their cars in a flash, a lot of shouting, and then they started fighting.

All of a sudden, local villagers appeared from out of the bush and started to rock the second car until they turned it over. Burt looked at me and said: "Turn around and get us out of here!"

After lunch, we tried again. This time, the traffic light was green and we sailed through – but not without noticing the car that had been turned over had also been set on fire and was now just a smouldering wreck.

This was my first time in a third world country and it was an eye-opener. Bad roads, no pavements, loads of locals walking everywhere and trying to sell you food, hairbrushes... You name it, there was someone who would run up to the car if you were waiting at a traffic light, hoping you would buy from them. Women with babies, young kids and people with no legs or arms begging... It was a lot to take in on my first day.

We had a staff apartment on the plateau where all the big hotels were located; it was where the expatriate management lived, and there were also expensive houses for wealthy locals. Here there were good roads and pavements and good shopping. We spent a couple of days opening wooded crates of equipment, filling the power units with hydraulic oil and diesel, and pumping grease to every nipple I could find. Weatherford had just signed a big contract with Phillips Oil, who had two jackup rigs offshore from Abidjan. The word was that the exploration to date looked very good and it may be another Ekofisk oil field.

Burt asked me if I knew how to run a Gator Hawk. I did; I had completed the course and run several jobs with them in the North Sea. I asked him which Gator Hawk I would be running and was told the 7⅝" version and I would be testing drill pipe connections. The idea is that the Gator Hawk is pulled around the outside of the pipe connection once the connection has been made up by the rig crew. The chamber opens by pulling air-operated levers and the internal rubber packer wraps itself around the pipe connections. Then a sequence of locking rams is operated by the technician, sealing the rubber packer tightly around the connections. The inside of the packer is then filled with water and pressured up by the unit's internal pumps; the pressure for this job would be 3,500 psi. I met the Aberdeen technician coming off the chopper – the guy I was relieving – and asked him how the unit was running. "OK, he said. "But it's done a lot of work and been on the rig for a long time without returning to base for a service," which, at the time, meant being returned to Aberdeen"

I arrived on the jackup, which was called Jack Frost; not a name you can forget. I walked into the accommodation and reported to the company man. Then I went straight out to check the Gator Hawk. What a pile of shit! I had never seen a piece of equipment in such a bad state as this. It would take a lot of spare parts from Aberdeen to fix it; really, we required a new unit from Aberdeen ASAP. I reported my findings to the company man and he started screaming and shouting at me. "Hey," I told him, "I just arrived on board."

He stopped swearing at me and said: "We can't sit waiting for a new Gator Hawk from Aberdeen. I want a list of spare parts and I need it now! We can't afford to have this rig on standby while we wait on a replacement Gator Hawk to arrive."

Now, being dyslexic, there's nothing worse than being pressured by someone in authority to put something in writing in a short time frame, and my head was swimming. I thought I had seen a Hawkjaw parts manual in the equipment container, so I made my way outside to check. Yes, I was right – it was a little dirty, but that was OK. I started making a list of the parts required to keep the unit functioning until a replacement would arrive from Aberdeen. I was starting to calm down – I mean, I had the spellings for the items we needed – but I had rushed putting the list together. I had the Weatherford telex number that the parts list needed to be sent to; you remember telex machines? I mean, this was 1980.

I took the list to the company man. He looked at the list and the first thing out of his mouth was, "What the fuck? You can't spell, can you? For instance, what does that say?" He pointed at a word on the paperwork.

I froze. "ECT," I eventually stammered.

"Well," he said, "is it ETC? Is that what you mean?" My brain still frozen, I just agreed with him. "I hope your fucking mechanical knowledge is better than your spelling – or I will be running your ass off this rig!" he shouted, thrusting the papers at me. Frustrated, I took the list to the radio operator to send.

The next morning I was on the pipe deck, still upset

by my encounter with the company man, when a chopper arrived and a guy got off carrying a red kit bag with the Weatherford logo on the side of it. He turned out to be from our Great Yarmouth base in the UK. His name was Phil and he had just finished a job on the other Phillips Oil rig; Burt had sent him out to help me. Phil had brought some spare parts that had been stored in a container in Abidjan so, after lunch, we started to strip down the Gator Hawk. We were lucky that the rig would be testing for a couple of days and then pulling out of the hole by breaking out a single joint, with the rest set back in the derrick in 90 feet stands. The reason they laid down a joint was that when they ran the stands back in the hole, we would be testing connections that hadn't already tested on the previous run.

A day later, they received a delivery of more spare parts via a technician who had hand-carried them on his return to Abidjan for his two-month rotation. Lots of work was done to get the unit ready to test the drill pipe when they were ready to run the stands back in the hole.

The job started off OK but gradually the shims on the door pins started to break and fall onto the rig floor; the hook and door rams also started having problems closing and locking around the pipe. We had to stop the job halfway through and come up with a solution. We undid the air and water hoses from the Gator Hawk and got the deck crane to lift it to the pipe deck; there is no hot work allowed on rig floors for safety reasons. The welder welded an old pipe chain tong handle to the door of the Gator Hawk and a metal ring on the end of the bar. The unit was lifted back on the rig floor and we had a meeting with the driller and his crew.

For the next pipe connection, the Gator Hawk was pushed onto the pipe and the cathead chain was attached to the ring end of the bar with a shackle. Three roughnecks pushed on the bar to close the door and the driller pulled on the chain to lock the hook ram around the pipe. We locked the door ram and pressured up to 3,500 psi and held the test for 60 seconds. Then the pressure was released and we pulled the lock ram into the open-door position. The driller then pulled on the chain that had been run through a pulley to open the hook ram, and three roughnecks pushed on the bar, allowing the Gator Hawk packer to open and come free from the pipe. This procedure was done to over 800 connections until a replacement unit arrived from Aberdeen a month later.

One thing you learn in this industry is you have to keep equipment functioning and finish the job; non-productive time on a rig can get very expensive. When you start calculating the daily rig rate, supply boats and all the other supporting service companies that are required keep the rig running, it can run to hundreds of thousands of dollars a day.

Job finished, Phil and I were leaning on the hand rails, looking out to sea, when we spotted an expensive fishing boat sailing close to the rig. We could see three guys on the back of the boat drinking cans of beer and – I couldn't believe my eyes – there was a giant manta swimming alongside the boat. One of the guys jumped on top of the manta and sat there for a couple of minutes before the manta decided to dive into deep blue water and the guy climbed back aboard the boat. They gave us a wave and slowly disappeared from sight.

That was not the only thing that brought a smile to my face during that trip. We had a new company man arrive on board and he turned out to be a lot nicer to work for. On his first day, he called us to his office and told us the testing programme would last about a week, so he had booked us on a chopper back to town. It was good to be back in Abidjan, sitting at a bar on the plateau, drinking a beer and people-watching.

Burt turned up and told us we had all been invited to a party on the change boat of Phillips Oil's new crew. There were lots of people on board the vessel – girls in bikinis and men in swimming trunks – and a good variety of food and drink to be had. The boat pulled away from the dock into deep water. The sea was like a millpond and so blue; it helped me to forget the past couple of weeks offshore and a good time was had by all.

The following day, Burt told me I was returning to Aberdeen. Being back at home after six weeks away, I managed to spend a week at home with my wife before I had to go offshore to the Beryl Alpha to run a 7" liner. However, I was back home again after only four days and managed to spend a week painting and decorating the kitchen.

Then I had a call from the office telling me to pick up flight tickets and money. I would be going out on a three-man crew, along with two technicians from Aberdeen. I was happy to find out they were Ginger and Ian. I had run a lot of jobs with these guys, and now we were all off to Mogadishu in Somalia, East Africa.

Mogadishu, Somalia

The next day, we all met up at the airport as our flight connections were within a couple of hours of each other. Aberdeen to London, London to Nairobi in Kenya, and then a short hop to Somalia. On arrival at Mogadishu airport, we collected our bags and made our way outside. A 70-year-old, white-haired American guy was holding up a sign with our company name on it. "Hi," he said. "My name is Bill. Follow me to the other end of the airport and we can board the plane that's taking us out to the rig."

On the tarmac stood a very old airplane, a 1930's Dakota DC-3. Bill announced that this was his plane and he was our pilot. I hadn't flown in one of these before and I thought it was a funny-looking thing. The first thing I noticed was the front of the plane was higher than the back; it sloped down to a very small wheel on the tail. Inside, the floor sloped about 45 degrees, so when you sat down you were looking upwards. Very weird. And there were only six seats; the rest of the space was utilized for storing equipment to be delivered to the rig.

The plane took off over a short distance and, once in the air, it levelled off and we were back to sitting upright. We flew for about 40 minutes, the Indian Ocean on the right side of the plane and on the left, miles and miles of desert. Suddenly we banked over to the left. Down below us was the land rig we would call home for the next six days. I couldn't see a runway though, only hard cracked sand; obviously it hadn't rained here in a very long time. But before we knew it, we were descending – this was confirmed by the fact we were looking up at the sky again – and had landed and were taxiing our way towards the rig site.

This time, we were working for ARCO Oil (Atlantic Richfield Oil Company) and, as normal, we made our way to the company man's office. Weatherford was not supplying the casing running equipment here; we would run the rig contractor's equipment. The power tong and power unit were manufactured by Weatherford Lamb and the elevator and spider manufactured by Varco. Most rigs have their own casing running equipment, but this was part of their contract with the oil company. We normally didn't use rig equipment unless something went wrong with our own gear, but this time there was only one set of equipment on the rig. We changed into our work gear and dressed the tong and elevators for 7" casing.

Later that evening, we were sitting outside our cabin in shorts and T-shirts. It was nice and warm and you could hear in the distance the waves hitting the shore. The tool pusher stopped to have a chat with us. He was wearing ankle-height leather safety boots and told us we shouldn't wear flip-flops outside the accommodation, as there were small black snakes in the sand and if they bit you, you could die. It must have looked very funny seeing three grown men bolt for the cabin door and fight their way inside!

The first thing the rig did when it arrived at the well

site was to drill a water well. The water would be used to mix drilling mud but, being drilled so close to the ocean, it had a high salt content. Taking a shower wasn't fun with salt water – it wasn't very refreshing – and we were given special soap to use, which was supposed to give a lather but your hair was left feeling like straw.

The following day, we started to run the 7" buttress casing (BTC). There was no stabbing board on the rig; instead, there were two wooden planks tucked across the corners of the derrick at different heights, one at 35 feet and the other at 40 feet up from the rig floor. The reason for having two planks was that the stabber needs to be able to adjust his height to be able to stab the pipe as joints are not manufactured to be exactly 40 feet long; to meet quality standards, the steel mill may have to cut off some of the ends of casing, making them different in length.

At the start of the job, Ginger and Ian were up the derrick, one on each plank. They were both wearing safety harnesses, just in case they fell off the plank; this would stop them falling to the rig floor. It was normal safety practice for a stabber to wear a retractable fall arrester with automatic recall, meaning in the event of a fall, the stabber would coast to a stop. However, Ginger and Ian were wearing static harnesses. If one of them fell, they would stop abruptly and dangle just below the board.

Anyway, things were going OK. We had a small problem with the 7⅝" elevator. Sometimes the elevator would move from side to side in the derrick; the derrick blocks were free-swinging rather than on tracks. If the slips closed, the driller would have to stop at the first stabber and he would put a metal bar into a slot in the elevator and pull down on it, allowing him to open the elevator slips again, which would then lock into open position. This elevator was very old and the mechanism holding the slips open was worn out, but we had to carry on like this.

When it was time for dinner, Ginger came down from the plank to eat and then relieved me on the power tong. I was in the galley when Ginger came in. He told me that Ian had had a bad accident. Apparently, the driller was lowering the elevator over the box connection when the elevator slips bumped the connection. Ian had tried to steady the slips with his right hand and they set with his thumb between the slips and the casing. To make things worse, the driller saw Ian waving his left hand around and thought Ian was signalling for him to pick up the string, so he did – Ian right off the plank. Ian was dangling in mid-air with his thumb jammed between the slips and casing, being pulled in half by his safety line. Ginger was quick to notify the driller about Ian's dilemma and he ran up the derrick to help Ian get his feet back onto the plank as the driller lowered the casing string. Ginger then opened the slips with a bar, freeing Ian's thumb.

"Where is he now?" I asked.

"He's with the medic – but his thumb was hanging off!" Ginger said.

That left Ginger and me to complete the job and we were back running pipe 20 minutes later.

In the morning, we handed in our service tickets to

Tony, the company man, to be signed. He wrote 'Good job' on our job tickets and told us that ARCO had informed the British Embassy that Ian needed a doctor to look at his thumb and that we should go to the embassy as soon as we arrived back in Mogadishu. We walked outside the company man's office to see the DC-3 landing on the sand.

Once back in Mogadishu, we took a taxi to the embassy and were soon being escorted to reception by a Royal Marine. We were asked to wait and, after 30 minutes, a secretary arrived with some bad news. The embassy doctor was not in the country but she had been in touch with the French Embassy and their doctor would take a look at Ian's hand. The French Embassy was only a short walk away; we left Ian with the doctor and went to book our flights home.

ARCO had made us a reservation for one night at one of the hotels they had an account with. We checked in and I went to my room. There was a bad smell. On closer investigation, I saw that the bed sheets were dirty and had skid marks! They hadn't been washed for some time. I put towels down on top of the bed when I went to sleep. Mogadishu was a war zone shithole and I couldn't wait to get the fuck out of there.

Later, we met up with Ian in the bar. He looked like he was in a lot of pain. He told us the doctor had said there wasn't much he could do with his thumb and that it may have to be amputated once he arrived back in Aberdeen. The doctor had cleaned up the crush injury and given Ian a tetanus shot and antibiotics, plus some very strong pain killers.

We had arranged to have a drink with Bill, our pilot, at the American Embassy Club. Being a member, Bill could sign us in without a problem. Bill had a contract with ARCO Oil for the one well they would drill in Somalia and then he would return to his base in Nairobi. He was a very nice guy and could tell a good joke or two. He told us some of the background to this war-torn country. Somalia's defeat in the Ogaden War strained the stability of the Siad regime as the country faced a surge of clan pressures. An abortive military coup in April 1978 paved the way for the formation of two opposition groups: the Somali Salvation Democratic Front (SSDF) and the Somali National Movement (SNM). Bill told us that, while we had been on the rig, there had been several clashes in the streets of Mogadishu, resulting in a lot of casualties.

The next morning, we arrived at the airport and checked in for our flight to Nairobi. We stood on the concrete next to where our Air Alitalia plane would park. The plane came into sight and was making its approach when suddenly the engines went into overdrive. The plane started to climb up again and circled the airport. Standing next to me was a good-looking blonde girl in her thirties who I had been chatting to; she was a reporter from the Wall Street Journal. She told me she was supposed to have left the previous day but goats had got onto the runway and the plane couldn't land and had to return to Nairobi! Fortunately for us, the next time the plane came around it managed to land.

Two hours later we were at the baggage carousel,

collecting our bags. We hadn't been able to book our flight to London in Mogadishu and we were told at the British Airways desk that flights were fully booked for the next two days. We confirmed our booking and I asked Ginger and Ian if they had credit cards, to which the answer was no. "Just as well I have one then!" I said, looking up at a big advertising board that said, 'Welcome to the Nairobi Hilton Hotel'. "Because that's where we are staying!"

We spent the next three days hanging around the swimming pool and local bars, and in the hotel, where the bed sheets were clean. I wasn't going to take any shit from Weatherford Management when I handed in my expenses. What a fucking nightmare of a trip.

Ian didn't lose his thumb. Aberdeen's Foresterhill Hospital managed to save it, but they couldn't straighten it, and to this day, it's bent over to the right.

I hadn't been at home more than a week when the phone rang. Ted Leslie, the base service supervisor said: "You're off to Argentina and we need your passport for a visa." I drove out to the base that afternoon and handed it in.

Argentina, Here I Come

Two days later, I met up with Hamish and Peter – yes, the Peter who stepped on the rake in Italy. Ted gave us our flight tickets and travel money and lots of heavy Weatherford 16" power tong spare parts; we had to split the parts up between us and pack them inside our offshore bags. I asked where our passports were and Ted said we would be met at Heathrow Airport by a visa agent, who would give us our passports stamped with Argentinian visas. He added that we would be met by the Weatherford Agent when we landed at Buenos Aires International Airport. No other information was given except that we would be running 9⅝" casing.

The three of us met up the next day at Dyce Airport to start the longest flight any of us had ever taken in our lives. Landing at Heathrow, we were met by the visa agent, who handed over our passports. Then we checked in at the British Caledonian desk and were told to stand to one side and that someone would escort us to the helicopter. "No wonder this is going to be a long flight!" I said to Hamish, but no – the chopper was taking us from Heathrow to Gatwick. First class treatment!

As I said, we were flying British Caledonian and I must say that the stewardesses wore the nicest uniforms I have ever seen: tartan hat, jacket and skirt with a white ruffled blouse. Whoever was recruiting these girls had a very good eye for attractive women. The chopper was nicely decked out in tartan too; it made the North Sea S-61 helicopters look really drab.

The flight to Gatwick took about 15 minutes; just about time to finish our glass of free champagne. We were not long off the chopper before we were boarding our transatlantic flight. The aircraft was a DC-10 – you know, the one with a big engine on top of the tail wing; yep, the aircraft that had had a few cargo doors fall off mid-flight... I consoled myself with the knowledge that they must have fixed the problem by now.

We were only in the air for two hours before we started to descend. The captain informed us we were landing in Madrid to pick up more passengers and fill up the fuel tanks for our 11-hour flight across the Atlantic Ocean to Rio De Janeiro. The Atlantic is the second largest ocean, covering approximately one-fifth of the earth's surface. We would be over water all the way, so if something did happen to the plane, we were basically screwed.

The seat belt light was turned off and we were told dinner would be served shortly. The meal arrived in a plastic tray. Hamish was sitting next to me; Peter had decided to claim a row of seats that was empty, as the flight was only half full. Hamish pointed at his salad and turned over the small tomato, which had green mould on it. "Watch this," he said. "We will get free drinks for the rest of the flight." He pushed the call button. One of the flight attendants came and Hamish showed her the mouldy tomato.

"Sorry about this," she said, as she picked up the tomato. "I will be back shortly." She came back very quickly, put a new tomato on his plate and walked away.

I couldn't stop laughing at the look on Hamish's face. "This isn't right! They should be sued!" he said.

"Hamish, the next round of beers is on you, mate," I said.

The lights in the plane had been dimmed. Now, unlike today's aircraft, where you have your own entertainment centre in the headrest of the seat in front of you, back in the 70s and 80s planes showed films on a big screen at the front of the cabin. They were shown via an overhead projector, and you plunged your plastic tube earphones into the arm of your seat to listen. We were pretty pumped up as the film was James Bond 007, *Moonraker*, with Roger Moore. The projector lit up with a bright white screen and all of a sudden Peter's hands were up in the air, making flying birds and hopping bunny rabbits! There was lots of laughter as the shadow on the screen became a man's head with his tongue poking in and out; Peter was on form.

We were halfway across the Atlantic when the captain made an announcement that we were at 35,000 feet and flying over a big lightning storm. It was a fantastic sight. I mean, we've all seen lightning before but we were looking down on it. It took us over an hour to fly over and was the best light show I have ever seen. Truly memorable.

We landed at Rio De Janeiro International Airport and most of the passengers disembarked. Two flight attendants came back to ask if we were getting off, and I told her we were flying on to Buenos Aires. "No," they said, "it's carnival week. You should spend a couple of days partying before flying on!" I explained that we were working and had a tight schedule to keep. Shortly after, a new crew and passengers came on board, all ready for the three-hour-and-twenty-minute flight to Argentina.

On arrival, we collected our bags and walked outside the arrival hall, where we could see a man holding up a big Weatherford logo. His name was Lucca and he was a freelance agent who had picked up this job from the national oil company, YPF, which was running the job. We started to drive out of the airport – but very, very slowly. "Why are we going so slow?" I asked.

Lucca pointed at a sign by the edge of the road that said, 'Max 5 mph' and then pointed at one of the military sentry towers. There was a soldier standing up there holding a large machine gun. "You don't speed within the airport if you want to live," Lucca said.

"Take your time!" was our response.

Lucca explained that he was driving us over to River Plate domestic airport for a flight to Tierra del Fuego in the south of Argentina. There, we would have a one-night stopover in a small town called Rio Gallegos before flying down to Rio Grande, where we would stay until the rig was ready for us. Then we would take a chopper offshore to the semi-submersible General Ernie Moscone to run $9\frac{5}{8}$" casing.

I wasn't kidding about this being a long flight time. We had been on the go for over 24 hours already and we still had to fly further to Rio Gallegos, which would take another six hours as it stopped everywhere.

We boarded the flight, which was full. I remembered seeing on TV and in films people boarding planes in South America with chickens and other live animals –

and here it was, in real life. Once we were in the air and at cruising height, the safety belt sign was turned off and Peter said: "I am off for a piss." As he walked down the aisle, he was smiling at people and saying, "Hi... Hi... How are you?" Eventually, he arrived at the toilet door and went inside.

Suddenly, we hit some bad turbulence and the plane dropped in altitude by about a mile. My heart was in my mouth and everyone let out a "Woo!" Then the plane went deadly quiet and we all looked at the toilet door. The lock was pulled back and the door opened. There stood Peter, who let out a greeting and brushed a hand down his wet trouser leg. The plane exploded with laughter as Peter returned to his seat.

We must have stopped off five or six times, with people getting off and on, before we reached the last stop, Rio Gallegos. There was a guy from the hotel holding up a piece of cardboard with our names on it. When we arrived at the hotel, we noticed straight away that no one spoke any English. We were given our room keys and decided to shower and then meet up in the bar. I was first in the bar and remembered from my first honeymoon in Spain that beer was called 'cerveza'. I ordered three bottles and sat at a table.

It wasn't long before Hamish and Peter joined me. Hamish said: "That looks good – what that guy's eating over there." It was a cheese toasted sandwich, and we all agreed we'd like one too. Hamish walked over to the bar. He caught the eye of the waiter and started to make hand signals, with his left palm out flat and his right hand waving it over as he mimed putting butter, cheese and ham on the bread. Then he placed both palms together and made a sizzling sound.

The waiter looked at Hamish and said, "Toasted sandwich?" Peter and I laughed so hard, I nearly fell off my chair. Turns out 'sandwich' is the same word in Spanish.

First thing next morning, we flew to Rio Grande. As planned, there was a young engineer from YPF to meet us and he introduced himself as José. We put our bags in the back of his pickup truck, which had two long antennas on the roof and a two-way radio inside. On the drive to the motel, I noticed that everyone was driving pickup trucks with CB aerials, and it seemed everyone was wearing cowboy hat, blue jeans and cowboy boots; it was like being in the Wild West. It was also obvious that someone called Schlumberger had this place sewn up: it looked like they were running all the electric lines, cementing and well testing in the area, and there was a fleet of trucks with their logos on – Schlumberger, Dowell Schlumberger, Flopetrol Schlumberger.

The motel was small but clean and only served breakfast and sandwiches. José told us that the rig needed one of us to fly out later that day to make repairs to the casing tong using the spare parts we had brought with us from Aberdeen. Straight away, Peter said he would go. Hamish and I said nothing. Hey, staying at the motel and drinking beer sounded good to us. It was five days before we flew out to the rig, but not before we had checked out all the bars and restaurants in town. Because a lot of foreign visitors stayed there, more English was spoken in Rio Grande. The food was good:

sandwiches for lunch, fantastic beef for dinner – you could cut the steak with a plastic knife and fork, it was so tender and full of flavour. There wasn't a lot to do in town but play pool, darts, sleep and eat. The TV kept showing news reports of glaciers breaking up because of global warming; we were very close to Antarctica, but I didn't understand a word of the reports as they were in Spanish.

The day came for us to go to work. José dropped us off at a bar at the airport and we went to the heliport. And there it sat: Mr Jake, a Sikorsky S-61L chopper. It had its name on the sides of the fuselage and white painted teeth at the front. Hamish and I got talking to the two South African chopper pilots, who were sitting having a beer. I asked why the chopper was called Mr Jake and we were given the helicopter's history.

On 16th May 1977 at 17:35 LT, a New York Airways Sikorsky S-61L helicopter Flight 972 had made the 10-minute trip from Kennedy Airport to the Pan Am Building rooftop helipad without incident. It had been idling for about one minute of a three-minute turnaround when the accident occurred. The right landing gear failed while the aircraft was parked, with its rotors turning. The aircraft rolled over on its right side and was substantially damaged. Four passengers had boarded the aircraft and others were in the process of boarding. The passengers and three crew members aboard received either minor or no injuries; however, of the four passengers who were still outside the aircraft waiting to board, three were killed and one seriously injured. A pedestrian on the corner of Madison

Avenue and 43rd Street was also killed and another seriously injured when they were hit by a separated portion of one of the main rotor blades of the aircraft.

The National Transportation Safety Board determined that the probable cause of the accident was the fatigue failure of the upper right forward fitting of the right main landing gear tube assembly. Fatigue originated from a small surface pit of undetermined source. All the fatalities were caused by the operating rotor blades as a result of the collapse of the landing gear.

Now, you're probably asking yourself how this chopper was now working for YPF. Well, I know I was. We were told that a guy called Jake purchased the chopper, dismantled it, took the parts from the top of the Pan Am building via a service elevator, and later put it back together – and named it Mr Jake.

We boarded, and it was evident this was not your normal North Sea chopper. There were curtains up at the windows, patterned carpet on the floor and flowers in holders on the walls. It was more like being in your living room.

We had been flying for about 20 minutes when the chopper started to lose height and banked over to the right. I thought we must be coming in to land on the rig, but no – out of the window I could see a fishing trawler and we were buzzing it. I could see the faces of the three fishermen clearly. They started to wave at us, so we waved back. I think they were drinking buddies of the pilots. Bizarre. We started to climb and carried on to the rig, where we landed on the helideck and the pilots shut down the engines. I had never seen a chopper this size shut its engines off on a rig before.

The door opened and, to our surprise, we could see a lot of people standing on the helideck. We walked out to be greeted by a line of people, including the YPF company man, tool pusher, driller and engineers, who all shook hands with us. We were welcomed like royalty! Peter was waiting for us in the radio room. "What was that all about?" I asked him.

"I don't know," he said, "but they did the same for me."

The company man didn't speak English so, for the rest of our time on board, we talked to his engineer, Carlo, who wasn't long out of university and spoke perfect English. We were told they had another day's drilling before they reached TD (Total Depth) and would be ready to run the 9⅝" casing. Meanwhile, we sat about the accommodation watching videos, sleeping and eating.

Now here's a first. I walked into the rec room and saw Peter and Hamish talking to a guy cleaning his gun. A gun on a rig! It turned out he was an Argentinian deep-sea diver. You would quite often see divers on semis, normally when a rig was arriving or leaving a location – but this one was cleaning a gun. It turned out he was a military diver and this is why he had a gun. I don't know if it had anything to do with the forthcoming Falklands War with the UK, but the rig was sitting pretty close to the Falkland Islands. I don't know if this had anything to do with him being aboard the rig and I didn't ask – because he was holding a GUN!

I noticed Hamish had a pink T-shirt on. "Did you buy that shirt in that colour?" I asked him. He said no, his mother had washed it on too high a heat, along with all his underwear and a new pair of red jeans – and presto, the washing all came out pink. Peter could see the top of Hamish's underpants. He pulled on them and the pants just ripped right off him. Peter put the underpants up to his nose, looked at the diver and said, "Let's fuck him." Hamish was up off his seat and running out of the room, screaming like a banshee, followed by Peter and the diver with his gun! Hamish locked himself in the toilet and the two of them came back into the room, laughing their heads off.

Next day, we rigged up the equipment and started to run the casing. Things were going OK; I was on the tong and Peter was on the stabbing board, 40 feet above my head. We had run about four joints and I could see there wasn't a mud pipe fill-up hose on the rig floor. I asked the engineer if he was running an auto-fill cement float shoe and float collar and he said they were, so we didn't need a fill-up hose as this cement equipment permits the casing to fill automatically while being run in the hole. The valve is always in the open position, allowing maximum filling of the casing as it is lowered into the well bore. The circulation may be established at any time during or after casing is run. The flapper-type back pressure valve does not become operative until a metal ball is dropped or pumped down. Like differential fill-up equipment, the shoe is activated by the same ball. From this point on, like differential fill-up shoes, the auto-fill cement float shoe acts as conventional floating equipment.

We ran another 10 joints and could see that the casing was starting to float up and down. The engineer decided there was a problem and he dropped the ball, rigged up the mud fill-up hose and filled the casing. Then, after about five minutes, we could hear what sounded like an express train approaching. All of a sudden, mud shot out of the casing! It looked just like a blowout. I ran for cover and then there was silence… except for Peter screaming: "What the fuck!!" I came out from behind the drawworks. Everything on the rig floor was covered in mud, all the way up to the top of the derrick. And then I saw Peter. He was covered in mud from head to toe.

Hamish let Peter down to get a shower and, after a clean-up on the rig floor, we were off and running again, this time filling the casing after each makeup. The job only took nine hours and the company man, engineer and drilling company were very happy with our services.

During dinner, I was sitting next to Carlo, who asked me where I was born. I told him South Wales and he asked if I knew there was a Welsh colony in Patagonia. He went on to tell me there were still many towns and villages that had Welsh names, and the Welsh language was spoken by around 2,000 people in the main towns, Gaiman, Trelew and Trevelin. Apparently, over 50,000 Argentines claimed Welsh descent and elements of Welsh culture still persisted in the area, such as the region's many tea houses serving Bara Brith cake. Rugby matches were still widely played in Patagonia and

Eisteddfod cultural festivals were organised by the community.

The next day, we left the rig on Mr Jack and boarded a flight to Buenos Aires, where we were met by Lucca. He drove us to our hotel and said he would meet us for lunch the next day. It was early evening and I met up with Hamish and Peter in the bar. I showed them a leaflet I had picked up at reception and asked if anyone was interested in going to see a show. Peter said he was going to have an early night but Hamish was all for it.

The theatre was not too far away but we took a taxi, to be on the safe side. The theatre turned out to be more of a club – and a seedy one at that. We were told to check in our jackets and led to a table, where we ordered two beers. The beers arrived and we were asked for a credit card. The show started. It was a troop dancing with boleadoras, a Native American hunting weapon made of two or more balls tied together with rope. They are used to down cattle or game by entangling their legs. There was singing and dancing and drumming, and it turned out to be a pretty good show.

It ended and two more beers arrived – along with two good-looking girls. They said they worked at the club and asked if we would buy them a drink; they ordered whiskeys and Coke. The Latin American girl was called Mercedes and the other, a blonde-haired, fair-skinned girl, was called Eva. Maybe her SS grandfather had run away to Argentina after WWII to get out of appearing at an international military tribunal... Well, maybe. Their drinks arrived and they turned out to be very nice to talk to – but at what cost?

I called over to the waiter and asked for the bill. Then I told the girls that we had to leave as we had a long flight the next day. The bill arrived and Hamish said we should stop a little longer. I showed him the invoice. "OK. No more," he said. We paid the bill, collected my credit card and our jackets and made a fast exit. The show wasn't the biggest part of the bill; it was the drinks, which came to around $150 – in 1980, that was a lot of money!

The next morning, I met Peter and Hamish for breakfast. At the table was a tall, very good-looking girl, around 21 years old. She was from Germany and her name was Bianca Bosch – of the Bosch Electrics family. Bianca had been visiting her older brother, who was setting up a manufacturing company in the north of Argentina. She was very pleasant. I asked if she worked for the family company and she said no, she was taking a gap year to see what she wanted to do. She said she needed to pack her bags as her flight back to Germany was later that afternoon, but I invited her to lunch and said that our agent was paying, and she said she would love to.

Lucca arrived on time and we all went to lunch at an El Gaucho restaurant, where they cook the meat over a hot open fire. Lucca ordered a set menu for the five of us, which came on a big wooden platter. I must say the meat was some of the best I have ever tasted. At the end of the meal, Bianca said: "Don't you like black pudding?" (If you don't know, black pudding is a kind of sausage made with pigs' blood.)

I said: "Yes, I love black pudding!"

"So where's the plastic?" she asked.

I looked at everyone else's plates and there were circles of plastic, the outer skin from the black pudding – but not on my plate. Yes, I had eaten the bloody plastic. I am glad everyone thought that was funny, especially when I said hello to the plastic the next day on the plane home.

Visiting Argentina was a great experience, but I now look back at the 60 hours of flight time and 10 days away from home for a 9-hour job and wonder why Weatherford hadn't sent a crew from America. But I guess back in the 80s, Weatherford wasn't that big a service provider in America. Lamb Industries supplied equipment to rig contractors worldwide and Weatherford had purchased Lamb mainly for their products and engineering. I guess also it was hierarchic, because all the Weatherford workers were Europeans.

Anyway... The flight home was uneventful, except for the passing of the plastic rings. I just wanted to get home to the family.

Back on the North Sea

I was lucky to get a week off before the phone rang and I was off again to relieve one of the technicians aboard the BP gas platform West Sol Alpha. I had to stay overnight in a hotel in Hull and take a chopper from the BP refinery early the next morning out to the platform. It was an old Wessex helicopter – the first I had ever flown on – and ex-RAF, by the looks of it.

West Sol Alpha was a very small platform and normally only had three people aboard: the OIM (offshore installation manager), radio/medic and the cook. The rest of the crew, like the electrician, welder and labourers, were flown out each morning at 8 am and flown back to Hull at 4 pm. However, now on board was a BP company man and drilling engineer plus a drilling workover contractor with seven personnel plus four Weatherford guys.

As soon as I walked into the galley, I was told that the table in the corner was strictly for the OIM and that you didn't sit there. BP was not very happy with Weatherford, as the previous crew had over-torqued the chrome tubing string and it had to be sent back to Great Yarmouth for the box and pin end threads to be re-cut. This was no ordinary tubing: it was a chrome string used in wells that had high corrosion; utilizing corrosion-resistant materials like chrome helped protect well completions from highly-corrosive fluids and prolong the life of the well. The big problem with running this type of tubing connection is that you have to run them slowly and not overheat the connections or leave deep tong die indentations, thereby reducing stress, distortion and galling. The tong used special low-marking dies and the make-up was monitored by Weatherford's Joint Annualized Make-up computer (JAM).

The crews were working six-hour shifts so everyone could eat and have a break. I got changed and went out to the small workover rig, where I talked to the tong operator and JAM technician. They told me they had 65 joints in the hole and to come back at 6 pm to start my shift. I returned at 6 pm and was told that they now only had 45 joints in the hole, because they'd had to lay down galled/bad connections. The problem is that when you have a bad connection, you have to also back out the connection above to be able to lay down the joint – and sometimes that joint galls on backing out, and so on. The job took us three days to complete and seeing the last joint being run through the rotary table and getting a good pressure test was fantastic.

We were released by the BP company man, who told us we were booked on the morning chopper to take us back to Hull. We had just finished eating breakfast when we heard the Wessex helicopter coming in to land on the helideck. All of a sudden, the whole platform shook. The Wessex had crash landed on the helideck above our heads! The platform alarms had been triggered and the OIM informed us over the radio to go to our lifeboat station and wait for further instructions. After about 10 minutes, the alarms stopped and we were told to stand down and go back to the accommodation. Well, we didn't get off the platform that day; in fact, we had to stay a further three days while a supply boat with two engineers and two new Rolls Royce engines were lifted onto the helideck. Apparently, the chopper's engines had just cut out as it came in to land. The new engines were fitted and the chopper was flown off the platform, with a Sikorsky S-76 coming to take us back to town. This is one of those times when I think I may have dodged a bullet.

The Israel Job

Ginger and I arrived at Heathrow Airport, checked in and were in the waiting room. I had worked with Ginger on a lot of jobs on the North Sea and, more recently, on the ARCO Mogadishu, Somalia job. The bus took us to the El Al plane but when we got off, we were told to wait for security checks before we boarded. There were two fit young guys: one inspected our flight tickets and passport and the other ran a metal detector over us. In those days, this was very unusual. Normally, security was very lax, but there had been several hijacks of planes to and from Israel and this was a necessary precaution. In fact, Israel was the first country to use sky marshals.

On arriving at Tel Aviv Ben Gurion Airport, security was very tight. You had to run the gamut of security personnel with questions like, "Where are you from?", "Why are you visiting Israel?", "How long will you stay?" and "Where are you staying?" A female officer said: "Is this business or pleasure?" Business, I told her. Then she wanted to know the name of my company and the company I would be working for in Israel. I told her and she gave me a blank pink card. I asked what it was for and she said: "Ask the passport officer to stamp this card instead of your passport." She went on to tell me that if I needed to visit an Arab country with this passport, I shouldn't have an Israeli stamp in it, as I wouldn't get an Arab entry visa.

Once outside the airport, Ginger reminded me that we needed to change our travel money. This done, we hailed a taxi to take us to our hotel. We checked in and were told by the receptionist that the hotel would not be serving cooked meals because it was Friday and their restaurants were close for the Shabbat – part of being kosher means observing Jewish law, and it is a huge violation of Jewish law to work or do business on Shabbat – but that we could have sandwiches.

The next day, we telephoned the number we had been given by the Aberdeen office. The company rep on the rig told us to stay at the hotel that night and they would send a car for us the next morning. Ginger and I decided to take a taxi down town. We had picked up some brochures and felt adventurous. Ginger had a reputation for being able to look after himself; he looked as if he'd been in a few fights and with that head of red hair, I bet he was the one to start most of the fights. He did like a good drink. Having said that, Ginger was very smart and a very good technician. I was always a little jealous of him. I mean, I was a closet dyslexic and had only read about five books in my life. It wasn't easy for me to read a page of a book. My eyes couldn't make sense of the words because my brain was telling them to race down the page and everything would just look like a blur; the only way to control this was to stare at the words and read them slowly – and even then, I would have to go back and read it again to make any sense of it. But not Ginger: he would read a book a day and if there was nothing much else to do, maybe he'd read two.

We arrived at the seafront and found it busy with

people. Ginger was never shy to talk to strangers and next thing you know, we were talking to young Israelis and finding out about life in Tel Aviv. Not all of it was good. They'd had some bus bombings in the town that week, and we learned that all young Israelis, both male and female, had to do military service at the age of 18, or later if they attended university.

We were told about a bar called the BBC Club, which was very close and safe to be in. The BBC Club turned out to be the place expatriates frequented and we felt at home as soon as we entered. We ordered some beers and Ginger put down some money on the pool table. There were two American guys playing and when they finished, they asked if we wanted to play a foursome and we agreed. It turned out that they were working on the same land rig we were going out to; they worked for a mud company as mud engineers. We had a couple of games and a few laughs. They were interested in who we were and where we came from but they didn't want to say too much about themselves.

After a good lunch of fish and chips, we headed back to the hotel. We met up again at 7 pm and ate at the buffet restaurant. Then we took our beers out onto the terrace. The temperature was perfect. We sat at a table and were approached by a tall, good-looking guy with platinum hair; I'd say he was in his early fifties. He asked if he could join us and sat down. He was a pleasant guy and said he worked for Mossad, the national intelligence agency of Israel. He asked all the normal questions – what we were doing here, where we lived and who we were going to work for. Now, this may sound a little paranoid but we were in a country that was, technically, at war. He bought the next round of drinks and by now he was already in our good books. He told us his name, but I didn't take much notice of it as I was pretty sure it wasn't his real name. He asked if we had driven out to the rig yet and we told him we were scheduled to drive out there in the morning. He told us you could see the Golan Heights from the rig location; he said he was in the army when the Syrians attacked through the Golan Heights in 1973, during the Yom Kippur War. He had some gruesome stories about that conflict and I must say I was glad I wasn't an Israeli; I would have been of the age that would have been called up for duty.

There was a hotel next door to ours and we could see that there was a wedding reception in full swing: disc jockey playing the latest pop songs and some old Yiddish dance music. Our new friend asked if we had ever been to a Jewish wedding and when we said we hadn't, he was up on his feet, saying: "Let's go." We walked into the wedding party and it was as if he knew them, so there was no problem with us gate crashing. We were handed some champagne and we watched the families and friends having a great time. After a few more drinks, we said our goodbyes to our new friend and made our way back to our hotel.

Next morning, we were picked up and driven for about an hour into the desert. We arrived at two big gates and there sat the land rig, in an area about the size of four football fields. The whole area was fenced off and along the top was razor wire; there were tanks and personnel carriers around the rig and military personnel in the lookout towers. We arrived at the company man's office and lo and behold, sitting in front of us was Tony, the ARCO Oil company man from the Somali job. He told us he was still with ARCO and that ARCO was in partnership with the state oil company, Zion Oil & Gas. He said he had asked for the two of us by name to come on this job as observers and that the $9\frac{5}{8}''$ casing would be run by the drilling contractor. I asked why he needed two guys to just watch the rig crew working and he told us he wanted to motivate them to run casing faster and safer. He wanted us to assist them in rigging up and operating the equipment and pass on some tips and tricks to the crew.

Tony told us to go and get lunch and take it easy until we were called later that evening. We made our way to the mess tent, which was full of army personnel eating their lunch. Leaning against the tent wall were machine guns put there by the soldiers. We took our place in line. Standing in front of us were the two American mud engineers we'd played pool with at the BBC Club. The first engineer took his tray to a vacant table. The second guy kicked one of the machine guns on purpose and they all fell like dominoes; probably around 35 guns fell onto the floor. The room went deadly silent. The engineer put his tray on the table and several military personnel got to their feet. The American just looked at them. He waved his hand downwards and the soldiers sat back down. "Let's sit on a different table," Ginger said.

We were eating our lunch when Tony sat down at our table. "Did you see what just happened?" I said.

"Those two are not just mud engineers," he replied.

"Don't have anything to do with them."

"Are they with the CIA?" I asked. Tony just looked at me and gave a little nod. Then he looked down and started eating his meal.

The job started at 10:30, when there was a short toolbox talk. Tony introduced us and said we were there to advise. It was obvious from the get-go we were not welcome. They didn't want us to run their equipment and I felt like a spare prick at a wedding. We did our best to help them, and I must say they weren't that bad at running their casing equipment, but their running speed was too slow because they were waiting on casing to arrive at the V-door. Ginger walked up to the drill floor and talked to the driller. "Look, there's plenty of space at the V-door for more than one joint," he told him. "Pick up three joints and that will stop you having to wait on pipe. There's plenty of room left in the V-door to put the elevator on without a safety issue." So this was done. We helped sling three joints together for the rest of the job and the running speed greatly improved; no more waiting on pipe. The job only took seven hours and Tony was very happy with our input. He signed our tickets with a 'Good job' in the remarks box.

We left the rig that day, and a car drove us out to Ben Gurion airport. Security again was very tight: both hold suitcases and hand baggage were searched and put through the metal detector, and then it was question time again.

This was my last job overseas as a technician. I worked the next few months in the North Sea, but still racked up 20 to 26 days a month. During 1980, I averaged around 20 days a month away from home, which Ellie and I had a few heated arguments about. I mean, it's not easy being an oilfield wife; it takes a special woman to cope with this type of life. In my case, all the monthly payments – house, car, insurance etc. – were taken care of by Ellie and if something went wrong with the house or the car while I was away, Ellie sorted it out. Not so easy while also holding down a full-time job. She had a supportive family and friends but a lot of marriages end up in divorce when the husband works away from home for so long, like I did.

The End of My Offshore Life

Christmas and New Year's Eve came and went. Of course, I was on a North Sea rig. Ellie spent Christmas with her mother and father and was at a party at my brother Haydn's house for New Year. We didn't know it then but by mid-January, I would be called into the office for an interview with Hartmut Hansen, the country manager for Saudi Arabia, for a sales engineer's position. The interview went well, but I was very concerned about how much paperwork would be involved. The paperwork I had to complete as a technician was very small: just fill in your service ticket book with the job information – which I had plenty of time to do with no one looking over my shoulder – and get the company man to sign it. Once in a blue moon, I'd have to send a list of spare parts via telex from the rig radio room and if I could, I would always try phoning the Aberdeen office and ordering the parts that way. I asked Hartmut if there was a lot of paperwork involved in the job as my spelling wasn't great but said that I was a good communicator and oil company personnel seemed to like me. Hartmut said he knew and that Bill Burnett, the Aberdeen base manager, had confirmed this. He added that, being German, his English spelling was also crap and that there were excellent secretaries in the Saudi office who looked after most of the paperwork. He told me he was interviewing two other guys and I would be notified by late afternoon if I'd got the job.

Ellie was OK with me taking an office job but it would mean she would have to quit her job with Schlumberger and she understood she couldn't work or drive in Saudi Arabia. I told her the monthly salary and that it would mean taking a big wage cut with only one salary coming in each month.

The phone rang around 4.30 pm. It was Bill, and he told me that Hartmut wanted to offer the job to me. After a few seconds I said: "OK, but I need to read the contract before agreeing to take the job."

I put the phone down and turned to my younger brother John, who was visiting us from Wales. "So did you get the job?" he said.

"Yes."

"Bloody hell, Les, you could look a little bit happier about it!" he said.

I collected the contract from Bill's secretary the next morning. She told me that Hartmut was on his way back to Saudi Arabia. I had arranged to meet Ellie in town to go through the job offer in detail. Over lunch, we discussed the contract. The salary wasn't that bad, but we would lose about 40 per cent of our combined income with Ellie not working. However, the company would provide a house and car and pay all the utility bills, and I would only need to pay a company 15 per cent tax equalization. We also knew we could rent out our house very easily as a corporate let and at a decent rate. We looked at each other and Ellie said: "Let's go for it. If we don't like it, we can always come home – but it's a life together and a start for you on the corporate ladder."

My passport was sent to the Saudi Embassy for an entry visa. I remembered to take out the piece of pink paper with the Israeli entry and departure stamps on it; I was glad the stamps were not in my passport. I also had to travel down to London to a Saudi-appointed hospital for a standard Aids test. This done, the hospital sent the results to the embassy.

The Corporate Ladder in 1981: Saudi, Here I Come

It only took 10 days to get my Saudi visa and my passport came back quickly. I arrived at King Abdulaziz Air Base with butterflies in my stomach. Would I be able to do the job? Yes, I was a good talker and liked meeting new people, and people seemed to like me too, but what if I couldn't do the bloody paperwork? I was told not to take any duty-free alcohol into Saudi Arabia as it was a dry country and it was against the law. Customs searched my luggage and it took over an hour to go through passport control; it was bad luck we had landed at the same time as two other jumbo jets.

Hartmut Hansen was waiting in the arrivals area for me. It was early evening and the weather was just right, nice and warm. We drove to Al-Khobar, arriving at the Al Gosaibi Hotel, where I was booked in for two nights – enough time for me to buy bed clothes, towels and kitchen utensils for my new house. I had been given one month's salary allowance to pay for essential items; other than that, the house was fully furnished.

The next day I arrived at the office and was surprised to find it was located in a one-storey house with a small sign outside saying, 'Weatherford Saudi Arabia'. Hartmut introduced me to the staff and showed me my office, which was what would normally be a bedroom. I would spend the next four years sharing this office with a Saudi sales engineer called Abdul. He wore western clothes and his English was impeccable.

As soon as I met Abdul, I blurted out: "How many wives do you have?"

"How many wives do *you* have?" he said.

"One."

"Funny, that. Me too."

"But you could have more than one wife," I said.

"Why do you think I want more than one wife?" he asked, cupping his hands over his ears. "What, fucking stereo?" and we both laughed.

I was given the key to the house I was going to move into. The office driver drove me to the house, which was just around the corner. It was a very plain one-storey building with no real garden, just three steps up from the steel gate and one and half metres of marble tiles around the outside. Once inside, you walked straight in to a large living/dining room; two bedrooms, a bathroom and a small kitchen all ran directly off this room. I could see the floor needed to be hoovered as fine sand, brought in by the air conditioners, covered everything. So I went back to the office to pick up a vacuum cleaner.

Now, if I had been an American, I wouldn't have made such an idiot of myself on my first day at work. I plugged the vacuum into a wall outlet and started to suck up the sand from the floor. At the time I did think the Hoover was making a funny sound, but it sure was sucking up the sand and I didn't think anything of it until flames started shooting out of the backside of the cleaner! I quickly unplugged it. The room was full of smoke. Back at the office, I told Hartmut what had happened and he said the Hoover was a 110 volt model and I had plugged it into a 220 volt socket and blown it up – and it was now fucked. I mean, in my defence, I didn't know the house had both 110 and 220 volt sockets dotted around the rooms. I didn't even know electrical appliances came with 110v motors; you don't see them in Europe. What a first day.

Across the road from my house was a supermarket that sold household goods, so I purchased what I needed and moved in the next day. The company government relations officer, who was also called Abdul, collected my passport to start the process of applying for my residence permit. Now, I knew I was blood group O positive and I even had my blood donation card with me but no, that wasn't good enough, and over the next week I had blood tests for my residence permit, Aramco Oil company ID pass and also for my Saudi driving licence – and yes, they were all O positive.

The next week, I was on the road visiting the Aramco drilling offices in Dhahran. Ras Tannura Offshore Drilling were located in the largest oil production terminal in the world, and the land drilling offices were located in Abqaiq, where Weatherford had their workshop. Aramco fed and housed our 40 international service technicians, who worked three months in the country and then had one month's home leave. We also employed TCNs (Third Country Nationals) as drivers and mechanics – 20 personnel from Pakistan and the Philippines – and they worked a one year on, one month off rotation. As for me, my contract stipulated two weeks' paid leave every six months.

I would be kept busy visiting 157 drilling rigs with some of the most difficult clients and the toughest climate I have ever worked in. I will share with you some of the good, the bad and the ugly times during my four and a half years living and working in the Saudi kingdom.

It took a little longer than expected for Ellie to arrive, because of visa bureaucracy, and this was to be the biggest challenge she would have to endure. It was difficult to come to terms with the idea that women in Saudi Arabia couldn't drive or work. Outside the house, Ellie had to cover her arms and legs down to her ankles; she needed a wardrobe of kaftans. There were no bars, nightclubs or cinemas; just the one Aramco TV channel and socialising at friends' houses – but, on the plus side, it was a great place to save money.

I was clocking up about 700 miles a week in my first company car, a Mazda 5 estate. Company cars had to have the company logo on both sides and on the back of the car, in both English and Arabic, and a vehicle fleet number; mine was WSA 5. I would normally spend one day in Dhahran, two days in Abqaiq and two in Ras Tannura, visiting drilling managers, superintendents and engineers. Most of the time I would be spreading the gospel; I mean, we had 100 per cent of the casing running business in Saudi Arabia, for there were no other casing companies in the country. I was involved with pushing new product lines and resolving job disputes...

And let's not forget the non-weld bloody centralizers... When I arrived, Weatherford and its Saudi partner Al-Rashid were building a small centralizer manufacturing plant in Dammam. The manager was Andy Jenner, who was also British. We were told at a meeting with the contracts department that Aramco didn't need any more centralizers as they had 50 years of stock in their warehouse in Abqaiq. The next day, Abdul Al Rashid met with Aramco executives in Dhahran and the outcome was Aramco would purchase 50 per cent of all centralizers in the future. Now that's when you know your partner is well connected with the House of Saud.

The day to day paperwork wasn't that bad. I had a fantastic Pakistani secretary call Khiam and he made my life a lot easier. I would scribble a telex on a notepad, having spent some time writing the letter with the help of my trusty battery-operated spell checker, and if he got stuck he would come to my office and say, "Do you mean this, Les?" and I would say "Yep."

I used to enjoy visiting the rigs on Tuesdays with the Aramco drilling superintendents. The Abqaiq superintendents would visit two or three of their rigs – sometimes we would fly to them and other times we would drive – and it was a great way to bond with them outside the office. It was the same with the superintendents from Ras Tannura: they would fly out by helicopter, again visiting two or three rigs each, and I would get a free lunch out of the visit. Driving onto an Aramco base was like visiting Little America. Greyhound coaches and yellow school buses roamed the streets; there were American schools and fast food restaurants, baseball pitches and football fields. And I knew all the superintendents' secretaries, who were all American women – yes, women; one law for Aramco and another for the rest of the international companies.

One day, I got a call from the land rig company man in Al-Hofuf: they were running 9⅝" casing but were having problems with our centralizers. Aramco's policy was to run a centralizer on the first 10 joints and every other surface, but this was a test well using the Weatherford wellbore wipers and scratchers I had sold to Aramco, and they had got stuck in the hole. It was a two-hour drive into the desert from Al-Khobar to Al-Hofuf and when I got there, they were running back in hole. All I could see around the bottom of the V-door were destroyed centralizers, wellbore wipers and scratchers. The company man told me the string just would not go down. He told me they had run the standard centralize programme and had run the same number of wellbore wipers and wellbore scratchers. I showed him my programme, which said to only run one wellbore wiper and scratcher on the first 10 joints, NOT to run them on every other joint to surface. The company man said, "You understand this never happened. We will throw the broken centralizers, wellbore wipers and scratchers into the mud pit, never to be seen again." Hey, I didn't care – they had come from Aramco stock and we had already been paid for them.

It was dark when I drove back. I had only been on the road for 30 minutes when I heard a big bang and the car came to a clunking halt. I lifted the hood and shone my torch at the engine. There was oil everywhere! I had blown the engine up, miles from anywhere. It was that dark you couldn't see your hand in front of your face. After about 15 minutes, I could see a set of car headlights in the distance, coming from the opposite direction. A battered pickup truck stopped and an old Arab man got out and looked at my engine. He could only speak a little English. I pointed in the direction he had arrived and said I needed to get to Abqaiq, but really, this was out of his way. I thought at best he would take me back to the rig but no, he told me to get in and he turned the pickup around and drove me to Abqaiq. I mean, how lucky was I? He drove me right to the gates of the Weatherford base. I handed him some money but he said no. I shook his hand and he was gone.

The Weatherford night supervisor gave me a pickup truck and I drove home, tired but thankful that I hadn't had to spend the night in the desert. The next morning, I was shitting myself about having to tell Hartmut about my car, but when I walked into his office, he just looked at me with a big smile on his face and said: "You were lucky that old Arab guy didn't kidnapped you!" The oilfield tom toms had already sounded and everyone knew.

If you have ever had problems with ingrowing toenails, you'll know this can be very painful. Appointment made, I was off to the doctor in Dammam to see what he could do for me. I arrived on time and was happy to see the building was fully fitted out with consultant rooms, an X-ray unit and an operating theatre. The doctor took one look at my big toe, which was infected and had yellow pus seeping out from under the nail. "Sorry," he said, "I have to remove the nail." He returned with a big needle and said: "You won't feel a thing." But he wasn't talking about jabbing the needle into my toe – oh no, he meant taking the nail off! Then, just as the nail was halfway off, the surgery doors flung open and a man lying face down on a trolley was rushed into the room. He had a large knife sticking out of his back. The doctor said: "I'll be right back," and he walked over to the guy and pulled the screens around him. So there I was with half a nail hanging off my toe, thinking only of myself. I mean, I didn't know how long it would take to remove a knife from someone's body and I would be in a lot of pain very soon once the injections wore off.

Eventually, the doctor returned and apologised for the delay. "Do you think I need more injections?" I asked. He shook his head and then ripped the nail off completely! I jumped about four feet off the bed. He bandaged up the toe, gave me a bag of painkillers and antibiotics and told me to leave before the police arrived. Abdul, our government relations officer, told me later that the local news reported that an Indian man had been stabbed on a building site and another man had been arrested. Fortunately, the stabbing wasn't fatal.

Along with Andy Jenner and Iain Fraser, the company finance controller, I purchased a water ski boat, which we used at Half Moon Bay. We would be there every Friday; in the Middle East, Thursday and Friday is the weekend and we worked Saturday and Sunday. This one Friday, Andy and Iain were out of country, so Ellie and two close friends of ours skied that morning. We were eating our lunch when, from the corner of my eye, I could see that the tide was coming in and our boat was floating away from the shore! I left them talking and tried to swim out to the boat but I didn't seem to be able to gain on it and I was getting very tired. I looked back and, to my horror, the current had taken me far offshore. I decided I couldn't catch up with the boat and started to swim back to shore. I am not a strong swimmer and I soon ran out of steam and started to panic. I sank, took a big gulp of water and went under again. The adrenaline was pumping and I thought: "This is it." I started to wave at people on the beach but they couldn't see me. I went down for the third time and thought: "I'm fucked!" Suddenly, my feet touched sand and I was able to crawl my way onto a sandbank. I was saved! With tears running down my face, I realised this wasn't my day to die. I was able to walk most of the way back to shore along the sandbank and only had to swim a short distance to the beach.

When I got back to the group, Paul asked me where I had been. "Trying to catch that fucking boat!" I shouted, and I walked off in the direction of the coastguard office. You had to register with them before you put your boat in the water and your boat's information was given to the coastguard patrol vessels. Any boat not on their list would be stopped for questioning in connection with smuggling from Bahrain: alcohol, drugs, guns etc. If you forgot to register, you stood a big chance of them confiscating your boat. As I reached the coastguard's office, I could see one of their patrol boats towing my boat back. I was given a right telling off and told not to let my boat drift away again.

My wife and I took a 10-day vacation, sight-seeing in Singapore, Hong Kong and Thailand. While in Hong Kong, we decided to try La Ronda, one of the best revolving restaurants in the world, and the only one in the city at the time. We arrived at the Furama Hotel on Connaught Road and took the lift up to the top floor, where the restaurant was. We ordered seafood soup followed by an Australian wagyu ribeye steak with French fries, and a good bottle of Australian red wine. The waiter came to the table and asked if we would like to look at the dessert menu. I asked if they served Irish coffee and he said yes, that was one of the things La Ronda was famous for. Two minutes later, the lights in the restaurant dimmed and the waiter returned with two glasses: one with whisky in it and the other with hot coffee. A sommelier stepped forward and set fire to the whisky. Then he lifted the glass as high as he could and tipped out the contents, aiming for the glass of coffee. It was a fantastic sight: a blue trail of burning whisky flying through the air. Except he missed the glass filled with coffee and the flaming whisky landed on the restaurant carpet and caught fire! Well, the lights came back on and the waiter and sommeliers started to put the fire out with their shoes. The head sommelier came over to our table and said he was very sorry that this had happened but it was the guy's first time; the sommelier who normally did this was not available as he got burnt last week. It was the funniest meal I have ever had and to this day, 40 years later, it still brings a big smile to my face when I think of it.

When we arrived back in Dhahran Airport from

Thailand, it took over an hour to get through passport control. We picked up our bags and made our way to the security hall for baggage checking. The guy in front of me lifted his suitcase up on the desk and the officer started to check through it. His bag was closed and he walk away, leaving a cardboard box on the floor containing a new radio cassette player. I lifted it up and was going to shout after him when the officer took the box from my hands and started to empty the contents; he even opened the battery compartment in the radio. Once we were through security, I made an effort to try and catch the man outside, but he had gone. Ellie was right behind me and she pulled on my arm. "Why did you pick that box up?" she said. "It could have been full of drugs!" I went very cold. If it *had* been full of drugs, there's no way the customs officer would have believed it wasn't mine. I mean, can you imagine spending 15 years in a Saudi jail? But hey, on the other hand, I got a brand-new ghetto blaster for free.

As I said, I used to spend two days a week visiting the drilling department in Ras Tannura and over the years I made some good friends. Bob, an engineer in charge of all Aramco casing cementation programmes, asked me one day if I would like a pork roast. Now, I bet you're thinking, *Big deal!* But yes, it was a big deal in Saudi to get your hands on any type of pork. Pork was illegal – you could only get it through someone working for Aramco – and there were long jail sentences and/or deportation if you were found with any pork-based product in your possession, unless you were an Aramco employee; they could buy pork but had to eat it on the base.

I picked up the pork roast at Bob's apartment and he said: "Hide it under your car seat. If you get stopped, you didn't get it from me."

As I drove back on the highway to Al-Khobar, I saw up ahead a police roadblock. I was thinking: "Someone has told them I have a pork roast in the car!" There was no way I could turn around now. I hoped I was just being paranoid. I pulled up to the policeman and wound down my window.

"Driving licence," he said. I handed it over. He looked at my licence, handed it back to me and said, "OK." Then he waved his hand and I drove off. I was a bath of sweat; it was like I had just got away with 5kg of heroin under my seat.

I got home from work one day and Ellie asked me if I would run her girlfriend home as her husband was working late and she needed to get back to meet the kids from school. "No problem!" I said. Pam jumped in the front seat of my car and we were on the Dammam highway before you knew it. The traffic started to slow down and we could see there was a police roadblock up ahead. "They probably just need to see my driving licence," I said – but we had a real problem because Pam was not my wife and she shouldn't have been sitting in the front seat! "If they ask me, I'll say you're my wife," I said. Fortunately, we didn't have to stop – they just waved us straight through – but if they had asked for both our ID cards and spotted the different surnames, we could have been deported.

After two years in Saudi, it was time to move on.

Hartmut, Andy and Iain had all been promoted and moved to other countries. Now Ellie and I needed a fresh challenge. I had been pushing my new country manager, Glen Gates, for a transfer at the end of my contract. However, my contract ended and I was told management were still working on it. Three months passed without a word, so I told Glen I needed to put my CV out to other companies as Weatherford weren't doing anything to relocate me.

One week later, I was told we were being transferred to the Philippines. The visa process began but then everything stopped because, on Sunday 21 August 1983, Benigno Aquino, a former Philippine senator, was assassinated on the tarmac of Manila International Airport. The door to my new job in the Philippines had been slammed shut.

It took a further four months to organise another job, as sales engineer for Weatherford Indonesia. Our friends threw us a few parties before we left. By the way, you always know where the party is happening in Saudi Arabia: it's the only house in the street with no cars outside. Expatriates have learned to play by Saudi rules, bending them a little but not so much as to draw attention to themselves.

We also held a party for our friends and Ellie made some eggnog from Sidiqi, or Blue Flame; we used to purchase this illegal 100%-proof alcohol for about $100 a gallon from a British guy working for Aramco in Dhahran. I had obtained a photocopy of a clandestine booklet called *Blue Flame*, which told you how to find out if Sidiqi was safe to drink. The trick was to set fire to a tablespoon of Sidiqi and if a red flame appeared, it indicated it hadn't been distilled enough and it could make you blind if you drank it. The Sidiqi from this British guy always burned with a bright blue flame, which meant it was safe.

The *Blue Flame* booklet also showed you how to brew alcohol using a pressure cooker with a temperature gauge welded to it. You added sugar and water to this home-made distillery and out came Sidiqi, or Sid for short: 100% neat alcohol that should be mixed with 50% water and left for 24 hours. Then you could add Coke or essence of juniper for ersatz gin. To make her special eggnog, Ellie had, by mistake, picked up a can of Sid that hadn't been mixed with water. But I must say it was one of the best parties we ever had and everyone had a great night falling about on the floor playing Twister.

Next thing we knew, the packers had been and gone and it was time to say goodbye – but not without me nearly having a heart attack at the airport. Just before we were due to board the plane, there was an announcement: "Would Mr Les Ellis please come to the British Airways desk?"

I walked up to the desk and a guy said: "Les Ellis?" I nodded. With a stern look on his face, he said: "I need your boarding cards." I gave him the tickets and he ripped them up and said: "You're not going." I had a big lump in my throat by this point. "Well, you're not going economy class anyway!" he said, handing me two red first class tickets. "My boss told me to tell you both to have a nice flight." His boss was Alan, a good friend of ours and the British Airways manager for Dammam airport.

We boarded the plane, sat in our first-class seats and, once the doors had closed, we were handed a glass of champagne. As we taxied out onto the runway, we made our escape in style.

Selamat Datang di Indonesia, 1984

After spending a month visiting parents, lawyers and cleaning our house ready for new renters, we were ready to start our new adventure in Jakarta. It involved a long journey: Aberdeen to London, and then the very first nonstop flight from London to Singapore, which took 13 hours. We arrived at Changi Airport, changed terminals and boarded the two-hour Singapore Airways flight to Jakarta. On arrival, we lined up to go through passport control. Eventually, we handed over our passports. The officer looked at them and said: "Stand over there."

About ten people passed through without a problem and then a British guy who had been on our flight walked over to me and said: "Go and ask him for your passports. Put five dollars inside and give him the passports back."

So I did, and the officer stamped our passports and said, "Welcome to Indonesia."

We had been allowed a small air freight shipment – TV, my Technics stereo system, bed sheets, some dishes, pots and pans, and knickknacks; our clothes were in four suitcases we brought with us. We came out of the terminal and were confronted by wall-to-wall people. It was a bit overwhelming after Saudi Arabia, but then, Jakarta is the capital city of Indonesia, with a local population of around eight and a half million. I had been told to look out for a man holding a board with the

Weatherford logo on it. There stood a short Indonesian guy, around 45 years old, holding the board. We shook hands and I couldn't help noticing his right-hand little finger had a very long curled nail. I found out later that long fingernails indicate someone is not a manual labourer but has an administrative or academic role. It was a tool to set them apart from the larger crowd of hands-on labourers in the professional arena.

The guy's name was Abdul Razak and he was my driver. He drove us out of the city to our new home in Pondok Indah. Our house was on a new housing estate with jungle to one side and the Pondok Indah Golf course to the other. Razak sounded the horn and two big steel doors opened to the parking area and a large car port. We drove in and the doors closed behind us. We got out and met our gardener, Wan, who was just 16 years old. He looked after a small lawn and a smaller Japanese garden surrounding a kidney-shaped swimming pool with a diving board. Standing at the front door was a pretty young girl, around 20 years old, called Samina, who was our full-time house maid. She handed us a letter from Jim Sayer, the Weatherford country manager, welcoming us to Indonesia and inviting us to dinner that night at a steak restaurant in town.

Inside the house, all the floors were of white marble. There was a very large L-shaped lounge and dining room and a toilet for visitors, two kitchens – one inside and one outside the house – and a big landing upstairs with three bedrooms leading off it, all with en suite bathrooms. The master bedroom even had a large balcony overlooking the swimming pool. I thought I had died and gone to heaven! The owners of the house were both doctors and had kitted the place out with basic furniture but after a few weeks our shipment arrived and we made the place look like home.

That evening, Razak drove us to the steak house to meet up with Jim and Ed, who was the sales manager – and also my boss – and Ray, the service manager, and their pretty Indonesian girlfriends. The beers were flowing and the steaks were very good. Everyone was telling jokes and having a good time. This was the life! I felt a little cheated, having spent three years in Saudi, but then again, it had been good training and probably helped me stand out from other candidates.

The next day, we ventured out for lunch in a local restaurant. That was fun. The menus were in Bahasa Indonesian and our first attempt at buying lunch was a disaster, with us both getting three main courses: Nasi Goreng (fried rice), this Nasi, that Nasi (that each came with a fried egg on top); we thought the last two should have been desserts! After that, we only went to restaurants with pictures of the food on their menus. However, it wasn't the case when you splashed out on the hotels and fine food establishments because the staff spoke English and you could ask for an English menu.

Monday morning arrived and it was time to go to work. I left the house at 7 am to get to the office for 8 am. There was wall-to-wall traffic and it was slow going but nice being driven; it gave me plenty of time to look out of the window and watch the thousands of people going about their daily lives. School kids in their different school uniforms, shop keepers opening their store for business, people crossing the road dodging motor bikes, cars and trucks. After 30 minutes, we entered downtown Jakarta, Jalan Thamrim, and drove into the Wisma Kosgoro Building, entering via the multi-storey car park entrance.

I walked through the reception area and into an elevator. The doors opened at the 6th floor and I could see the glass doors in front of me and a sign saying 'PT.Wiri-Insani' (Weatherford). I was feeling apprehensive about what to expect. Jim introduced me to the Indonesian staff: secretaries, accounts department and my fellow Indonesian sales engineer, Edward, who was a young guy with perfect English and a permanent smile on his face. What a difference to the office in Saudi. It was like chalk and cheese, because all the secretaries and accounts staff here were female. Indonesia is the largest Muslim country in the world but the women are liberated and can work, drive cars and work for western companies. Some women wore headdresses, most were dressed in western clothes and all spoke good English.

Jim, Ed and Ray had their own offices and I shared with Edward – but our office had a good view up and down Jalan Thamrim. The Russian Embassy was cross the road and I used to wonder what the employees were up to: probably sending out top secret messages via the big satellite dishes on the roof. I was given a file with a list of customers. Most of the big oil companies operated here, both onshore and offshore. I looked through the contracts we held with clients for both TRS and products like – yes, you guessed it, centralizers. The next thing I knew, my phone rang and Jim said: "Let's go for lunch."

We entered the elevator and, to my surprise, we went up to the next floor. The doors opened and I was astonished to see a pub! With its thatched roof and white walls with inlaid black wood battens, it looked like a traditional old English house. This was the company watering hole. It was called The Shakespeare, the inside was finished in the style of that period and the waitresses all wore lace hats and short gingham dresses with white lace aprons. As for the food, there were all sorts of grilled meats, burgers and chips, and the bar served a wide range of alcohol to wash it down. This was a place where we would meet clients at lunchtime and after work. If you were entertaining clients, you would put the invoices on your monthly expenses report, along with their name and the company they worked for, and you were reimbursed, no questions asked.

At this time, the price of oil was still very high and the industry was booming. I was told by Jim to entertain clients and their wives, while he, along with Ed and Ray, who were single, would take care of entertaining the single clients. This involved taking them to places like The Hole in the Wall and The Black Hole, where you could look through a one-way mirror, watch girls promenade and choose the number she was wearing; there were lots of establishments like this dotted around the city.

It wasn't long before Ed found out about my product expertise. I was now in charge of all the centralizer and float equipment tenders – yep, off his desk and on to mine. I was concerned at first, but product tenders are mostly about numbers; I only had a problem with reading and writing if someone was looking over my shoulder, and I can tell you this didn't happen. No one wanted anything to do with these tenders and anyway, most of them already had the product descriptions. I just filled out the boxes with numbers and added product brochures. With no one breathing down my neck, the rest I could handle, no problem, and I soon got very good at tenders.

Ellie was starting to settle into life in Jakarta. She enrolled in a Bahasa Indonesian class and after a month was talking like a native. But then, she was very good with foreign languages and got on with people easily. She had made friends with clients' wives, which led to coffee mornings; she joined groups like the St Andrew Scottish Society and became part of the Highland dancing group. She also started to help out with one of her friends at an orphanage; I know she wanted to start a family of her own but we'd had no success yet. It wasn't long before she got a job as the PA to the Charge d' Affaires at the British Embassy. It was not a highly paid job, as Ellie was employed as a local employee, but we did get membership to the British Embassy clubhouse, where there was cheap beer and fantastic fish and chips. We were also invited to a lot of nice parties at the ambassador's residence.

The embassy was two buildings down from my office and across from the famous Hotel Indonesia, immortalized in the film *The Year of Living Dangerously*, about a love affair in Indonesia during the overthrow of

President Sukarno. The film follows a group of foreign correspondents in Jakarta on the eve of an attempted coup by the 30 September Movement in 1965. I was told that Sukarno had a hit squad that would roam the streets of Jakarta looking for men with tattoos on their arms that might link them to this group. Thy would be arrested and put in oil barrels, which were then filled with concrete and dropped off the back of a boat or thrown out of a helicopter into the South China Sea. I had seen a lot of old men in the streets with very scarred arms and Edward told me they had burnt off their tattoos to prevent them from being murdered.

I was starting to travel around Indonesia, to places like Balikpapan, where our main warehouse and workshop was located. Weatherford also had a service base in Medan, to service Mobil Oil's contract, and a third base in Badak 4, a drilling camp located in the middle of the jungle; equipment came from the Balikpapan workshop.

I enjoyed visiting clients in Tanchang Berou and Pekanbaru too. Trips would last between 5 to 10 days and they were always very interesting places to visit. Pekanbaru was right on the equator – half the town was on one side and the other half on the other side – and this is where I had my first encounter with an earthquake. It only lasted a few seconds and was not bad enough to damage the building, and I don't believe anyone was killed – but it was still a little scary.

Highlights and Lowlights
of My Stay in Indonesia

One night, Ellie had gone to bed not feeling well and had been sick and had diarrhoea throughout the night. I got out of bed to check if she was OK, but she was looking very pale and couldn't move. I touched her face, which was very cold, and I pinched the skin. It felt like putty and I realised she was very dehydrated. Jim and Ed were out of town, so I phoned Ed's girlfriend, Merry, and she said she would come to the house right away. It was Sunday – my driver's day off – and my car was always left at my house, so I decided to take Ellie to the Pertamina Oil Hospital; I passed it on my way to work so I knew how to get there, and Merry would do the translating when we arrived.

It was Sunday, early morning with no traffic on the roads, so it wasn't long before we got there. Nursing staff came out of the emergency room, put Ellie on a gurney and pushed her inside to where a doctor was waiting to examine her. He inserted a needle in the back of her hand and hooked up a saline drip. Then he took a blood sample.

I heard an ambulance arrive outside with full sirens going and a lot of talking, which got louder as they entered the room with a small boy, no older than 8 years old. The doctor and nurses tried to resuscitate the boy but within minutes they stopped and everyone left the room. A couple of minutes passed and the doctor checked the boy's vitals again and then tied a label with the boy's name on it onto one of his big toes. He was dead, lying about two metres away from Ellie's bed. No one came to put a sheet over him, and he lay there peacefully in only his red swimming trunks. Merry later told me that he had been staying at the Hilton Hotel and had drowned in the pool. Security staff had tried to save him but they were too late.

Ellie was admitted and told she had dysentery, probably from some crab meat she had eaten the evening before. They recommended she have a full medical check-up once she was back in the UK, but she was out of hospital within three days and back to work after two weeks. Expats enjoyed health care as part of their contracts and we were covered by Bupa so there was no problem with having to pay for medical treatment.

Talking about medical treatment, it was my turn to have a medical problem dealing with... Yes, it was my ingrowing toenail again. Actually, this time both my big toes were badly infected. I visited the company doctor and was passed on to a plastic surgeon who specialised in big toes. His office was located in the Phillips Oil building. I shuffled into his reception wearing carpet slippers with the front of the upper part removed so there was no pressure on my toes. The receptionist told me the doctor was waiting for me in his office. I opened the door to the surgery and walked in. There was no one there. Then the door closed and I looked around to see a little Indonesian guy in a white coat who had been hiding behind the door! *Funny*, I thought. He examined my toes and asked if I'd had problems before and I told him that the left toenail had been removed in Saudi Arabia; I didn't tell him about the guy with a knife in his back. He said that taking the nail off was not a long-term solution and that he needed to remove 1 cm either side of the toenail down to the nail root. I was in so much pain he could have cut the bloody toes off, for all I cared! So he started with injections into the top of the toes and then he removed the roots. Within half an hour he was bandaging them up. He told me to come back the following week and I walked away with lots of painkillers and antibiotics. I still reported for work each day, but I must have raised a few eyebrows as I entered the lift and parted the crowd so I could stand at the back with my back to the lift doors. I wasn't going to let anyone step on my toes! A week later I was back at the doctor's surgery and again there was no one to be seen. I looked behind me to see the door close with the doctor hiding behind it. The little guy was weird but, forty years later, I haven't had any problem with ingrowing toenails.

We were woken one night by loud bangs that made our windows shake. I opened the balcony doors to see in the distance a large fire and explosions, missiles shooting off in all directions, and what sounded to be machine guns firing. Then we lost the power to the house – but this happened a lot in Jakarta, especially if we were having a thunderstorm. But this was no thunder storm! The noises went on for the rest of the night and once or twice we heard a loud whistle and bang close to our house. By daylight, there were no loud bangs, just the odd noise like fire crackers going off. I received a phone call from a mate in BP who told me that he, along with other BP families on his compound, had been evacuated because of a fire at a nearby army explosives warehouse. Mortars were landing too close to his house! The fire was reported on the news, and there had been a few fatalities.

Indonesia was ideally close to a lot of places you could visit during the many national holidays they had each year. One time, we took a short flight to Bali and chilled out for a few days. I didn't know we lived so close to Paradise. We were just back from Bali when Jim called me to his office. "Les, I just got a letter from your old friend Paul," he said. Paul was a guy I worked with in the North Sea. Jim handed me the letter to read. Now, I would normally freeze at this point, but it was in large writing and not very difficult to read. It said: *Jim, you cunt, you fucking cunt, I have been stuck up in Badak 4 for over six months, you cunt, and I need some R&R, you cunt. Paul.* Jim said, "Well, if nothing else, he got straight to the point!"

"I guess Paul needs a little time off in Scotland!" I said, and we both burst out laughing. One thing I learnt in this industry is that technicians are like time bombs, just waiting to go off.

The months were rolling away. During my ninth month in Indonesia, Jim was called to a budget meeting in Singapore with the regional manager, the VP for Asia and the CEO of the company, who was visiting from Houston. He returned to Jakarta to pack his bags – they had demoted him to sales manager in Aberdeen. Apparently, half the Indonesian budget was based on a contract with Krakatau Steelworks and there was a problem with the supply of American Aero water blasters. American Aero was a subsidiary company owned by Weatherford, and the water blasters were to be used to clean the inside of one of Krakatau's blast furnaces. However, because of delays in putting the furnace down, we were showing a huge loss on the books. With my eight years' experience of working for British Steel, I knew you only put a blast furnace down when you couldn't patch up the interior brickwork any further and this was why the job hadn't started.

The new country manager arrived and right from the get-go we didn't hit it off. Peter was a Dutch Indonesian – in other words, he was of mixed blood; he grew up in Holland and was very smart. Did you know that Dutch ships arrived in Indonesia in the late 16th century and colonized the country until the declaration of independence in 1945? This is why you see a lot of Indonesians living in Holland. Peter had been working as a sales manager for Oil Tools in Jakarta at the time Jim left, so he was in the right place at the right time and was hired on the spot; he didn't even need to be rehoused. I asked him and his wife to dinner and all he could do throughout the meal was complain! We had a micro switch on our water tank and every time Samina turn on a tap or a toilet was flushed, the switch would completely fill up the tank instead of filling to a certain level; the system required a new micro switch, which would save electricity. Throughout the meal, Peter kept telling me to get it fixed and I kept saying that the company would have to pay for it as the rental contract didn't cover this expense. His face went bright red and he told me I should pay for the work and that it should have been done a long time ago. I was mad! I told him to read my contract as it stated the company would be liable for all utility costs.

After that, the writing was on the wall for me, because Peter wanted to replace me with another local salesman. He hired an Indonesian sales guy from his old company, a chubby short guy called Indra, who was about 30 years old. Indra was known by Edward, who didn't have a good word to say about him except that he and Peter were as thick as thieves. To make things worse, Peter was a big mate of Bob Hendrix, the regional manager.

We were at home one weekend when the phone rang. Ellie said: "It's Hartmut. He wants to talk to you." I hadn't talked to Hartmut since he left Saudi two years earlier; he was now the Weatherford Regional Manager for the Middle East, based in Dubai. He told me he was in Bali for the annual regional meeting and could he stop over as he needed to talk to me about a job. I thought to myself, *This must be in Dubai.* He arrived at my door the next morning and told me he had just handed in his notice with Weatherford and had taken a job with an American company called Frank's Casing and Rental Tools. Started by Mr Frank Mosing in 1938, Frank's had moved recently to Jakarta but was a very small player internationally; in the states, it was the biggest TRS company. Hartmut went on to tell me he was now the vice president for the Middle East and would like to hire me as his sales manager. The contract sounded good and

I knew I needed to leave this job – but I had only completed 12 months of my 24-month contract. But Weatherford probably wouldn't transfer me and I knew I was in for an unpleasant 12 months working for Peter. So I said yes. Hartmut returned to Dubai and, four days later, I received my signed contract via courier.

Now the fun began. I handed in my notice to Peter the next day. He looked through it and said: "You know you haven't completed your contract? You will have to repatriate yourself, as Weatherford will not pay for that."

"Let's see about that," I said. "I mean, I have worked eight years for this company without a problem." Peter just shrugged his shoulders. I was a bit shocked that he hadn't asked me why I was leaving or where I was going; after all, I had been very successful with winning tenders and solving client service problems in Indonesia.

Ed came over to my desk and said: "That's a good move, Les." I asked him if he'd had any problems with Peter, but I already knew the answer. Ed stood two metres high, weighed 110 kg and was German – and he could be really nasty if he wanted. His ace in the hole was that the top management at Weatherford were all German – and to boot, Ed was a frightening fucker.

I gave Ellie a call at the embassy and told her that Peter said he wasn't going to pay our flight ticket or our furniture shipping costs. She said she would have a chat with her boss and phone me back. The phone rang 30 minutes later and Ellie told me her boss had advised her to write a letter to Weatherford informing them that they couldn't leave us stranded in Indonesia and that they were responsible for our repatriation to the UK. Ellie told me to collect the letter in half an hour.

I handed Peter the letter, which was on British Embassy stationery and signed by the Charge d' Affaires. If looks could kill, I was dead. He said: "I will run this past Bob in Singapore and get back to you." The next morning, Peter told me the company would pay for flight tickets back to Aberdeen but only the equivalent cost of the air shipment I sent to Jakarta from Saudi – and this would be paid to me in my last salary payment. I pointed out that I had four weeks' vacation left and as I had to organise my shipment and sell Ellie's car, I would need two weeks to stay at the house and utilize the company car and driver; I would forfeit the other two weeks and have the balance added to my last payment. He agreed to this deal.

Ellie's Suzuki 4WD was only nine months old, low mileage and immaculate, and was quickly sold. We had been very happy with Samina's work and asked her if she was interested in working for us in Dubai. We offered her double the money and four weeks' vacation after 12 months, and a flight ticket home, and she agreed. But then we found out that she had been working in Jakarta without a work permit – the Government only gave out a limited amount of permits to control the number of Indonesians living in the city – and she also didn't have a passport. I was very friendly with Edward, our Indonesian partner's sales manager, who I'd had many beers with in the Shakespeare. Edward was very connected with government departments so I visited him on the 8th floor of our building. He told me he knew a military general who could fix the work permit and the passport problems and he would set up a meeting.

The next afternoon, Edward and I set off to a kampong in the city centre. We entered a nice house right in the middle of the kampong. In the front room were two secretaries sitting at desks. Edward explained in Bahasa that we had a meeting with the general and we were shown into his office. The first thing I noticed was a guy cleaning a hand gun and weird-looking bullets on the desk. We shook hands with him and were asked to sit down; his English was very good. I could tell right away that Edward and the general were good friends; apparently, Edward was the agent for Remington Guns and Ammunition Company for the Indonesian military. We discussed Samina's permit and passport and the general said there would be no problem sorting it all out. We agreed on the cost, cash on delivery.

Being very nosy, I asked the general what type of bullets he had on the table and he said, "These are HP (hollow point) ammo for my 9mm pistol." I asked about the rifle on the wall, which looked like a wire coat hanger, and he said, "This is a one-round assassin rifle. It is very light and disassembles very quickly – and weighs nothing."

I said – and I really wish I hadn't: "Is it accurate?"

He got up from his seat and took the rifle off the wall. "I'll show you." Then he walked outside into the busy kampong. "Do you see the lightning conductor on the building next to the Hotel Indonesia?"

"The Phillips Oil building?" I said.

"Yes," he replied, and he adjusted the scope on the rifle. Now, remember the kampong was right in the middle of skyscrapers. He fired the gun and, unbelievably, hit the conductor on the Phillips Oil building. You could see it move. He turned around and put another bullet in the gun and, with his arms out, said, "Do you want a shot?"

"No!" I said. "I would probably land up killing someone." The general and Edward just laughed. We went back inside and the general told me to bring Samina to his office the following day at 8.30, and that one of his agents would take us to the offices to get the permit and passport sorted out. He added that Samina should be wearing white for the photos.

The next day, we turned up at his office at 8.30 on the dot. Samina was wearing a white T-shirt and white slacks. One of the girls asked us to sit down and said the agent would be here soon to collect us. All of a sudden, we heard a man and a woman's voices coming from one of the back rooms; they were screaming at each other. Then the woman started shouting, "No, no!" BANG. A gun went off and next thing, a woman ran out of the room towards where we were sitting, clutching what was left of her left hand. Blood was spurting everywhere; some came Samina's way and she moved just in time to stop it landing on her clothes. The middle-aged woman, who I think was the general's wife, ran out into the kampong. We looked at the open door and then the general appeared in the doorway, wearing only boxer shorts and a white string vest and with a gun in his hand. My mind was racing. *We need to get the fuck out of here,* I was thinking.

Then a young guy – the agent – walked into the office. He looked at the blood on the floor and the girls told him, in Bahasa, what had happened. He looked at us and said: "Let's go before the police arrive." He didn't need to tell us twice – we were out of there!

We arrived at a photography shop, where some passport photos of Samina were taken. Then we went to the permit office, where Samina signed the necessary paperwork and the back of her photos. Then off we went to the passport office, where she did the same thing. The agent told us he would handle the rest; we were free to go home and he would bring the permit and passport to my house in two days.

Two days later, I heard a car sounding its horn outside the gates. It drove in and I went out to meet the agent. He handed me the permit and a new Indonesian passport and I gave him an envelope with the cash payment. I said to him, "Is everything OK at the office?" and he told me everything had been sorted out.

The rest of the week was spent helping the packers with our shipment, putting stickers on the boxes addressed to Frank's Casing Crew and Rental Tools Dubai UAE. I had the flight tickets from Peter to Aberdeen: economy, one way. I took them to a travel agent and paid a small fee to have them altered so we could stop over for two days in Dubai. This would allow us to drop off four large suitcases and meet up with Hartmut before leaving for Aberdeen, where we would spend Christmas and New Year before returning on

January 5th.

Just before we left the house, we gave a good bonus to Razak, Wan and Samina. We also gave her the new passport and enough money to live on while we sorted out her Dubai visa.

Welcome to Frank's Casing Crew and Rental Tools, Dubai, 1985

Hartmut Hansen was at the airport to meet us and had arranged two visitor visas. I had been to Dubai once before for a Middle East sales meeting when I worked for Weatherford Saudi Arabia, so I had a good idea what to do to get through passport and immigration. On the drive from the airport, Hartmut told me we would be staying at the Middle East managers' house near Safa Park. We crossed over the Dubai Creek and headed for the Trade Centre Building; at the time, this was the highest building in Dubai and you couldn't miss it as we drove over Creek Bridge. The Trade Centre was right next to the Hilton Hotel and back then you had to navigate a big three-lane roundabout that sent you off to locations like the Sheikh Rassid bin Al Maktoum Port. We took the exit to Jebel Ali and Abu Dhabi; about half a kilometre up the dual carriageway on the right-hand side was the Ramada Hotel. We turned off the dual carriageway to the left, veered off into the desert to the next tarmac road and drove onto the Safa road.

We would be staying for two nights at the house of Dick Rader, the Middle East manager; he was away collecting his wife and two children from Houston and wouldn't back until the following week. We stored our suitcases in the maid's quarters and took our hand luggage to our room. That night, Hartmut and his wife Caroline collected us for dinner. We went to the Ramada

Hotel and sat in the Red Lion Pub; I mean, you could have been at home – it was decked out just like an old British pub and the place was humming with expats and Arab locals. This was no Saudi Al-Khubar in any shape or form and we reminisced about our time in Saudi, both good and bad. Before leaving the bar, Hartmut told me that that Mr Frank's grandson, Keith Mosing, would be arriving from Houston early the next morning and would also be staying at the house. Together with his father Donald, Keith ran the international side of the company.

I woke up early the next morning and told Ellie I was off downstairs to make us some coffee. I entered the kitchen to find a guy not much older than me sitting reading a newspaper and drinking coffee. I guessed straight away this must be Keith, so I said: "Good morning! I am Les Ellis."

He looked at me and said, in a deep Texan/Louisianan accent, "Keith Mosing. So who do you work for?"

For a minute, I was stunned, and then I blurted out: "You, I hope! I have just given up eight years working for Weatherford to become your new sales manager."

Keith just looked at me. Then he said, "There's a new pot of coffee if you want some," and went back to reading his newspaper.

When I got back to the bedroom, I told Ellie what had happened. "I am not sure I have a job," I said. After showering, we went downstairs but there was no sign of Keith. We ate breakfast and heard a car horn outside. It was Hartmut, waiting to take us to the office. We climbed into the car and the first words out of my mouth were: "Do I have a job or not?"

Hartmut looked at me. "What are you talking about?" he said. I told him the story and Hartmut said: "Keith knows all about you. He's pulling your leg, don't take any notice." But I had a funny feeling that Keith hadn't been told the whole story, if any.

The office was in a new building over the IBM showrooms; two apartments on the first floor had been joined together with an archway leading from one to the other. This created a spacious office, two kitchens, two bathrooms, two large living rooms and four bedrooms/offices, with plenty of room for expansion. I met the two British secretaries, Margaret and Sue, and our accountant, Pam, a Filipina married to an American working for Arco Oil as a drilling superintendent. Hartmut handed me a box containing a hundred business cards in English and Arabic with my name and job title. "Looks like I have a job!" I said, relieved.

Then he gave me the keys to Dick's car. "You and Ellie should take a drive around, maybe have a look around the gold souk and take a long lunch." We returned later that afternoon and only Pam was working. She said Hartmut and Keith were visiting clients and that we should take the car back to Dick's house and leave it there. A taxi had been booked to take us to the airport at 7.30 pm for our flight to London.

Knackered, we arrived back in Aberdeen, took a taxi home and crashed out. We awoke to a bright sunny morning but the temperature was below zero degrees. Ellie had a medical appointment at St John's Hospital, set up a month before leaving Jakarta. After her medical and blood works were over, the doctor said to me: "Do you feel OK?" I said I did, and he turned to Ellie and said: "Does he get easily upset and lose his temper?"

"Oh yes!" she said.

The doctor then said, "I would like to examine you, if that's OK." He checked me over, took my blood pressure, felt my throat and examined my eyes. Then he said: "You have an overactive thyroid." He explained that I had all the symptoms – gaiter in the neck, bulging eyes, loss of weight, bad temper – and said I needed medication right away as it was affecting my metabolism and would, ultimately, cause a deterioration in all my vital organs if it was not dealt with now. He took blood works and asked me to see my GP at the end of the week for the results. And he was right: my GP said I should really have an operation ASAP to take away part of my thyroid. I told him this was not possible as I was starting a new job in the next few weeks, so I was proscribed Thyroxin tablets and beta-blockers to control my thyroid.

We had a good Christmas and New Year visiting family and old friends, but it was soon time to board the plane for Dubai and a future with an up-and-coming international company – and, hopefully, a chance to grow with the company. Dick was standing outside arrivals holding a sign with my name on it. He was a tall, well-built guy, tanned and with blond hair. "Hi!" he said, with a big smile. "Welcome to Frank's." He dropped us off at our new home. It was further down the road from Dick's house and very close to the Chicago Beach Hotel, now the site of the Burj Al Arab Hotel; in the distance you could just see Jebel Ali Hotel. Located about 30 yards off Safa Park Road, it was one of four houses surrounded by desert. The only thing growing was a date tree – and, tied to the tree, was a goat with big horns. Inside the house was a large living room, kitchen, bathroom and two bedrooms; out the back was a wet kitchen and maid's quarters. We were pleased to see our sea shipment had already been delivered and the packers would be back tomorrow to unpack the boxes. This house was in no way as good as our Jakarta house but it was new and had no garden or pool to take care of – plus I didn't have to pay 15% tax equalization anymore. Dick handed me the keys to the house and a set of keys for a brand-new white Mercedes E90, which was sitting in the carport. We were off to a great start.

The next day, I reported for work and Dick drove me out to see where Frank's TRS equipment was being stored. It was in a corner of a warehouse belonging to another company that Frank's rented space from. I met four American technicians who were working on the equipment, young guys who had been transferred from bases in Texas. Frank's was working on one rig for Crescent Oil and one for DPC (Dubai Petroleum Company). It was early days – and, as sales manager, it was my job to get more work. Fortunately, the oil industry was still blowing hot and oil prices were over 100$ a barrel.

Dick suggested we get some lunch and we arrived at the Hilton Hotel. To my surprise, Hartmut, Keith and a third guy called Maxi Gremillion were waiting for us. Lunch went on all afternoon and a good time was had by all. Keith didn't say anything about our last conversation and that was fine with me.

The next morning I had a meeting with Maxi, who turned out to be the VP for worldwide operations. He was a very easy-going guy and we hit it off from start. He handed me a business card – but not his; it said on it 'Andy Jenner, engineering manager'. Maxi said: "You know this guy?"

"Yes," I said. "We worked together in Weatherford Saudi Arabia. Andy's a very smart guy."

"Okay," Maxi said. "It's just we have never heard of him. Thanks."

I walked out of the room thinking, *What in the hell is Hartmut playing at?* Yes, as a Weatherford VP you could hire anyone you wanted, but this was not a PLC corporation, it was a family company and I had been told by Dick that nothing was done unless it was first run past Keith.

During my first four months, I was busy visiting clients and learning about Frank's and its equipment. Frank's manufactured their own TRS equipment – power tongs, power units, CAM, a computer monitoring system and even some elevators – and, as Donald Mosing, who designed and engineered the equipment, said, "Our TRS equipment is not like Weatherford's. Our equipment is built for service, NOT for sale."

We were halfway through the year when, one morning, I was called into Dick's office. He told me that Hartmut was no longer with the company and he was the new regional manager. I didn't ask too many questions but I gathered Hartmut and Keith had some disagreements over how the company was being run. Dick told me I was going to relieve John Benoit, the country manager for Egypt; he was going on vacation for four weeks and I would cover his job. I would have liked to take Ellie with me but shortly after we arrived, she had started working for DPC, so that was out of the question.

The following Friday I arrived at Cairo Airport and an old Nubian guy met me; he was John's driver, Mr Ali. I had been interested in Egypt for a long time. My first wife Jacky and I had lined up outside the British Museum in London in the summer of 1972 to see the Tutankhamun Exhibition. We had queued outside the railings for four hours, only to be told by the police that anyone outside the grounds of the museum would not get in that day, so we had to put up with Madame Tussaud's waxworks instead.

I would be staying in John's house, but I was first taken to the office to meet John and the office staff. John ran through the contracts and the rigs he managed, and the number of Egyptian technicians that were working for him. He explained he had two cam technicians on loan, a guy named Randy from Texas, and I knew the other guy from Dubai; his name was Mitch and he was a bit of a space cadet but he knew his job. They were both out on a rig and should be back in about a week. John's house was just behind the American school where his wife worked as a teacher. She and his two kids were already back in Houston.

John left the following night and I was left in charge. I needed to make sure everything went as planned and there were no big surprises for him when he got back. Miss Femi was the office manager and she really ran the place – she was in charge of sending out the technicians to the various locations, materials and accounts, so my job was pretty easy. Each morning, Mr Ali picked me up at the house at 5 am and we drove over to see clients on the other side of Cairo, near the pyramids; this was also where our equipment containers were located. My first port of call was the Odeco drilling radio room, where I would check in with each rig to find out the status of our crews. By 6 am they would lose all communication, with their rigs being blocked by the military communication radios until evening. Then I called in on Exxon and had a chat with the drilling team, and by 9 am we would make the slow bumper to bumper two-hour journey back to our office in Maadi.

One morning, we were stuck in traffic on the Qasr El Nil Bridge. All of a sudden, a train of over 50 camels stampeded between the cars, chased by Bedouin-looking men with big sticks! It brightened my day, especially as I managed to snap a few photos of the stampede because I didn't think anyone would believe my story.

The second weekend, I visited the Egyptian Museum and stood looking at the Tutankhamun Exhibition in amazement. I was the only one in the room and I thought back 13 years, when I was standing outside the British Museum with hundreds of disappointed people – but not today.

Mitch and Randy arrived back the following week and we decided to visit the pyramids of Giza. It was a hot day but very windy, and that made it bearable. We followed the other tourists inside Khufu, the Great Pyramid, and on to the Sphinx. We watched people riding camels and horses and then we walked away from the crowds until we were outside the smallest of the three pyramids, Menkaure. We were approached by an old Egyptian who asked if we would like a tour around the outer buildings that were out of bonds to tourists – and we all said we would.

Finishing the tour, the guide said, "Would you like to climb the pyramid? You can do it, for a small amount of money that I will split with the security guards." This worked out to be around 10$ and we agreed. Mitch and Randy were wearing shorts and I had on jeans. They hopped up the large stones like mountain goats; each stone was about 30 inches high and covered in fine sand. Halfway up, I scraped my shin on the edge of one of the blocks. It hurt like hell and I sat on the edge of a block and pulled up my trouser leg. Blood was pouring down my leg! By now, the other two were at the top, shouting at me to hurry up. Heights don't worry me – after all, I'd worked on the derrick, on the monkey board and stabbing board – but this was higher and very slippery with no hand railings. Looking down, I could see the guide waving at us to come down and the two guards looking the other way. And coming down was just as hard as going up because of the slippery steps. We paid the guide and yep, I have dined out on this story for many years... but I think I was punished for climbing the pyramid, because it took three months for my leg to heal! It got infected and I had to go on antibiotics.

One morning, I wrote a telex to Dick informing him that Dubai had sent me the wrong tong dies and to send replacements. Miss Femi brought back the telex and said: "Shouldn't this word 'rong' have a 'w' in front of it?"

I went cold. I hated being caught out like this but, in a split second, I said: "Yes, but I don't use it. It's like knife: why should we put a 'k' in front of the word?" Being dyslexic, I must have made thousands of spelling mistakes, but being caught out hurt, and after that, I always put a 'w' at the front of the word 'wrong'.

Before I knew it, John was back from his vacation and happy to find out that there were no dramas waiting for him. Before I left, he asked me if I would stand in for him over Christmas and New Year, as he needed to take some time off then. I said that was fine if Dick was OK with it and my wife could come with me. Returning to Dubai, I checked if Ellie could get 10 days off during Christmas and New Year. That was sorted and I was happy to get a second chance as relief manager and to show Ellie around Cairo.

Now this was not the first time and wouldn't be the last time that, because of a shortage of technicians, I had to go on a job. The next time it was a land job in Pakistan. The job was running 4½" tubing for Flags Oil, a Canadian company. You know when someone says, "Where were you when John F Kennedy was shot?" This time it was "Where were you when the Chernobyl nuclear power plant accident happened?" Yep, I was on a rig in the middle of nowhere, somewhere outside Islamabad. I had visited Islamabad a couple of times before and found it to be a fascinating place, with lots of Russian army personnel running around the city, probably on leave from the war in Afghanistan, Pakistan being right next door. I used to stay at the Holiday Inn and you would see a lot of dubious characters hanging around. I once saw Geoffrey Howe – a fellow Welshman and, at the time, the UK Secretary of State for Foreign and Commonwealth Affairs – having dinner with a group of, as I said, dubious characters.

One evening, I went over to the bar in the American Embassy with a couple of my American technicians to have some beers and play pool. I was at the bar ordering the beers and there was a guy sitting at the bar, looking as if he had had a few beers already. He said, in a loud British accent, "Hey! I know you!" A table of marines looked over; they seemed to know him. "Hey, I haven't seen you since that incident in El Salvador!" By now, the two guys playing pool stopped to listen to what was being said.

"No," I said. "You must have me mixed up with someone else."

"Yes," he said, waving his hand about. "I paid for the drinks with American dollars." Now this was weird, because in all embassies you paid for food and drink in their currency.

My mates asked me what that was all that about. "I don't know," I said. "Let's drink up and go back to the staff house for a few drinks." Over the years, I learned to keep a low profile and not associate with people like him – or there could be consequences.

My next trip was to Jordan to meet with the national oil company. I stayed at the Sheraton Amman Al Nabil

Hotel, close to the embassy and business district, which had a history of terrorist attacks. Amman was very green with a lot of agricultural land; it was a nice change from the UAE deserts I was accustomed to. I was driven around by our agent and given a guided tour of Amman, but the sales visit was a bust. The meeting with National Petroleum Company (NPC) went well – they had plans to drill a lot of gas wells – but they had no money to drill them. I was told Frank's would be put on their tender list for future TRS work.

Driving around the Arab Emirates had its dangers: camels. Camels loved to stand on the tarmac roads at night because the desert nights can be very cold and this was a way of keeping their feet warm. The roads in UAE are very long and boring and you would find yourself driving at well over 100 miles an hour at times. Ultimately, you had a problem seeing camels standing on the road until it was too late. The camel's body is the right height that when a car hits it, it will come straight though the windscreen, with the driver being pushed into the back seat and killed outright. On two occasions I came very close to death, just missing the camel by inches. It's a known fact that more oilfield workers are killed in road accidents than on oil rigs.

Talking about camels, we used to borrow elevators and slips from three stacked Santa Fe land rigs park opposite my house. I would drop off a case of beer now and then in return for them helping us out with slips and elevators. George, the Canadian rig manager, was in his mid-sixties. He told me one morning, while I was looking for two 9⅝" single joint elevators, that he was retiring.

Dick and I decided to take him out for dinner and Dick thanked him for helping us out with equipment. Then he asked him what he would like as a leaving present. Straight away, George said: "A Ferrari!"

We both blurted out: "No!"

"OK," he said, "how about a road sign with a camel on it?" The next day, Dick and I purchased a red triangle with an outline of a camel in black on a white background.

George took one look at it and said: "No, I wanted a camel with big lips!" He had seen them for sale in a sign shop in Abu Dhabi. So I spent the next day in Abu Dhabi, going from shop to shop, and eventually I found a sign with a camel with big lips. We delivered it to George and he was so happy with the big-lipped camel, which he said would be placed at the bottom of his driveway in Alberta.

I had worked for Frank's for a year now and I'd had a much better time working for a family company than a PLC. Weatherford management were all European, whereas Frank's was American. They were a lot easier going but they wanted their pound of flesh... Keith told me once that you needed to employ more Indians than chiefs as chiefs didn't make money, and Frank's ran lean and mean compared to the likes of Weatherford. But I'd had more fun in that year than in the whole of my oilfield life to date.

Normally, I would be out entertaining clients with Dick five nights a week and deals were done at the dinner table. One time, a client dropped a copy of one of our competitor's tenders on the dining table and we were told to beat it by a dollar. Mr Frank's had a policy to treat the drilling engineers like superintendents and superintendents like drilling managers; when you did that, you found their doors were wide open all the way through their career.

I have always had a problem with ball blindness, whether it was golf, squash, tennis or softball. Frank's had two softball teams: Frank's Casers and Frank's Tigers. The Tigers were made up of the best softball players and most of them were our American clients. I, of course, played for the Casers and I was benched most of the time unless we were short of players. Frank's had built a softball pitch right next door to the Ramada Hotel and Red Lion pub. We used to get a good crowd at each home game and one of our best supporters was Larry. The oilfield was built with characters like Larry. He was a loud Texan who worked for Arco Oil as a drilling superintendent but, like a lot of people in this business, Larry had made millions in deals, lost it all and then made millions more; Larry was on his third time around.

One night, we had made arrangements to meet Larry for dinner at the Hilton Hotel. He was known to arrive late and go home late but he was good fun to be around. This night he was an hour late and when he arrived, you could see he had just finished lunch with someone; he was as drunk as a skunk. We were on our second pitcher of iced margaritas and also feeling good. We all ordered T-bone steaks with mashed potatoes and gravy. Larry picked up his knife and fork and started to cut his steak. Suddenly, he fell, face down, into his mash. Dick and I just looked at each other for a few seconds and then I said: "He's going to drown unless we do something!"

Dick said: "No, no, he's breathing. Look, there are bubbles of gravy coming out of his nostrils."

All of a sudden, just as quickly as he went down, Larry came back up with a big smile on his face. "Boy, that tastes good!" he said, and we all burst out laughing as he wiped the mash and gravy off his face with a napkin.

The year 1986 was not a good year in the oil patch. The price of oil hit $10 a barrel and work was starting to dry up; we were having to send technicians home. It was mid-May and the weather was getting really hot. Dick came to my desk and said: "I am going to get my hair cut. Do you want to come?"

"Yep," I said, "I need to get my hair cut too." Part of having an overactive thyroid is you sweat a lot and it was time to get a crewcut.

On the way back to the office, Dick pulled the car to the side of the road and just sat there, saying nothing. Then he blurted out, "I have to let you go."

"What?"

"You can stay on as a technician and get a housing allowance. We are haemorrhaging cash."

I knew things were bad, but not to that extent. "No," I said. I wasn't willing to go back down the corporate ladder.

It wasn't all bad news though. Ellie was glad we were returning going back to Aberdeen; she knew she could get a job pretty quickly, having talked to a few friends about the job market there. And, sure enough, she soon found a job with the French company Total Oil. We had to tell Samina that she had to go back to Jakarta – she had settled in well and her English had improved, but I think she was also happy to return home. And Ellie and I had been trying for a family but, having had no luck, we needed to see a specialist to find out what the problem was.

During our last vacation home, we had sold our cottage and bought a quarter of a mansion, Tillycorthie Mansion House in Udny Green, about 12 miles northeast of Aberdeen, and the first mansion built of granite and flint concrete. The part we owned was the lower west wing. It had a 70-foot hallway that ran the length of the house, with eight double wooden and glass doors leading into an area covered with a glass roof that we shared with our neighbour, who owned half the mansion. It was huge, with a big water fountain in the middle and indoor parking for eight cars. You're probably wondering why two people would need a house this big. Well, Ellie didn't; it was all down to me. I was brought up on a council estate in South Wales and, growing up, we never had much money. So I was showing off to my family and friends that this thick kid, who left school at 15, who no one thought would make much of himself, lived in a mansion.

After seeing our local GP, we were referred to gynaecologist Patrick Steptoe, who pioneered IVF work and made possible the birth of Louise Brown, the world's first 'test-tube baby'. We arrived at his clinic in Cambridge and while Ellie was being examined, I was led to a small room with lots of porn magazines. I did the deed into a glass jar, left my sperm sample on the table and returned to the waiting room. We were asked to go and have lunch in town and come back at 2 o'clock.

We entered Mr Steptoe's office and he gave us the results of the tests. "I can't see any problems with you," he told Ellie. "The reason why you are not getting pregnant is your husband." My sperm count was very high but the sperm were not good swimmers and died very quickly. In other words, I was shooting blanks. I sat there in a state of shock. My three brothers all had children. Why not me? So now I was dyslexic *and* infertile. Mr Steptoe ran through our options and we returned home with lots of pamphlets to ponder over. Ellie wasn't keen on adoption and I was not keen on someone else's sperm, so the subject was put on the back burner.

Before we left Dubai, Dick had told me that Frank's would send a retainer payment of half my monthly salary up to September when, hopefully, things would have improved. He called to tell me things hadn't improved and that Frank's had to stop the payments, but he would be in touch as soon as they had new contracts.

I had been spending lots of our savings on an idea I had to do with video advertising in airports and shopping malls. I registered a company call AVN – Advertising Video Network. I had seen video advertising on small TV sets in local airports in Jakarta and on large video walls placed on roadside structures in Dubai, and I was in love with the idea. I wanted to supply video advertising in Heathrow and contacted companies like Adshel, who owned 80% of static adverts on bus shelters all over the UK. However, after a few calls they said they weren't interested and it seemed no one else was either.

I visited my doctor for my annual blood test to see how my thyroid was coping with me taking all these tablets. He told me that the levels were still too high; he was going to refer me to a specialist at Aberdeen Foresterhill Hospital. Frank's had kept me on BUPA medical insurance so I got to see Mr McDonald the following week. After he examined me, he said: "You need a thyroidectomy to remove part of your thyroid as soon as possible. Are you busy at the moment?" I told him I didn't have a job at present so I was free anytime, thinking it would take a long time to get a date for surgery. "What are you doing next Tuesday?" he asked. When I told him I wasn't doing anything, he said, "OK, we will operate then. Report to the hospital at 8 am and we will operate at 10.30. You will need to stay in hospital for five days."

So there I was, lying in a hospital bed, waiting for my operation. I could see Mr McDonald walking towards me with four medical students at his heels. He picked up my chart from the end of the bed and said: "Good morning. Are you ready for your haemorrhoid operation?"

"No!" I said. "Wrong end!" and they all started laughing.

"Right," he said. "Good job you pointed that out."

I awoke from the operation to find Mr McDonald standing by the bed. "How do you feel?" he asked me. I couldn't talk, as I had a big tube down my throat. "It's good news," he continued. "We only had to cut away 73% of your thyroid and you don't have cancer." *Cancer?* I thought. *No fucker told me anything about the chance I could have cancer!* But hey, it was good news.

A couple of days after I returned home, I got a call from Ian Fraser, who had transferred from Weatherford Houston back to his old job as controller for Weatherford UK in Aberdeen. He had heard from someone that I was just out of hospital and wondered how I was and if we could meet up for lunch. We met at the Dyce Skean Dhu Hotel that day. I met Ian at reception and we walked through to the dining room, where I ordered fish and chips. It was great to catch up with Ian and find out what he and his wife Mary had been up to since leaving Saudi. My throat was still swollen and very sore, and as I took a mouthful of food I started to choke. I couldn't swallow – the food was stuck in my throat. I started to panic. I got up from the table and ran out to the toilets, where I looked at myself in the mirror above the wash basin. I was going blue and I could feel myself getting light-headed. I knew about the Heimlich manoeuvre but you needed someone to do it to you. Instead, I took two steps backwards and ran into the sink top, which was the same height as my waist. The food came out of my mouth like a bullet. Tears were streaming down my face when Ian burst through the toilet door to see what was going on. I ate soup for the next two weeks, but still choked if I didn't chew my food properly.

It was December and I had spent too much money on a broadcast video camera and editing equipment. I was going to media night classes at Aberdeen Art College each week and making some friends in the media business. With me spending all our savings on my new business, which was going nowhere, Ellie and I were having problems – but I am like a dog with a bone and I don't listen to reason. Aramco used to give its 25-year employees a Rolex 18ct gold Day-Date President Oyster watch as a reward, but the Arab employees just wanted to sell them. I had purchased one, complete with its leather box and a guarantee, from an Aramco broker for $2,500; in 1983, this was half the price it cost to purchase in the UK. And now there was no other way: I had to sell my Rolex. I advertised it in the P&J newspaper for £3,500. The first phone call was from Customs and Excise in Aberdeen, asking lots of questions about the history of the watch. I told him the story and he was happy that it wasn't a fake and wished me luck. Apparently, they scan the media looking for contraband and I had been red-flagged! The second call was from a used car salesman in Inverness and the watch was sold on the spot. Now, 39 years later, the watch is a classic and is worth over £40,000. Hey ho.

We were into the middle of January before the phone rang and it was Dick in Dubai. "Hey," he said, "we need you back ASAP. We have a big contract with Japex Oil Co in Abu Dhabi and we want you to be sales and operations manager."

With AVN, my video business, I was just starting to make contacts in some of the major oil companies to make safety induction videos, and I had all the video gear and knowledge of the oil industry to be able to produce films like this. So I said, "Can I call you back later? I need to talk to Ellie before making a decision." Things had not been great between us lately and I knew

Ellie wouldn't want to leave Aberdeen again; she was happy with her job and had made new friends. But we needed the cash, so I said I would go out there to make some money and maybe I would just rotate.

I phoned Dick back two hours later and said that I would come for three months and then see if we could make a deal on a three months on, one month off rotation. Dick said: "OK," and I heard laughter in the background.

"Who's that?" I asked.

"Keith Mosing," Dick said. "We had a bet between us. Keith said you would phone back within 30 minutes and take the job and I said two hours. So I won."

The deal was that I would go out for three months and open an office in Abu Dhabi – on the same salary as before, but on a single man travel and housing allowance.

Frank's Dubai, 1987

My first job back with Frank's Middle East was to meet up with the JPO drilling manager in Abu Dhabi. The Japanese manager told me he and his engineers would like to inspect the casing and tubing equipment before it was sent out to their rig, so we arranged a time for the following Sunday for the inspection. I made reservations for lunch for five at the Hilton Hotel after the inspection, and Dick had everyone painting and servicing the equipment. The workshop and yard had never looked so clean.

The Japanese team arrived dead on 11 o'clock and Dick and I showed them around. They asked lots of questions and we informed them that all the power tongs and power units were manufactured by Frank's in Lafayette. The last piece of equipment they saw was the Frank's CAM system (Connection Analyse Make-up) and I knew they were very interested in finding out how the computer derived its torque and turn evaluations.

Standing next to the CAM computer set-up was Mitch, one of the guys who climbed the pyramids with me in Cairo. Dick turned to Mitch and said: "Mitch, tell them about the CAM system."

There was a long pause and then Mitch said: "It's good. Fucking good!"

Dick looked at the drilling manager and said, "There you have it. Let's go to lunch."

I have to tell you that while I really felt at home in

Dubai, I didn't like Abu Dhabi at all. The Abu Dhabi oil company personnel weren't as good to work for. Adnoc Opco, ADMA Opco and Zadco were the biggest oil companies and wanted everything for nothing. In turn, Weatherford and Al Masaood had, over the years, driven the price down so low to get volume work, it made it tough to make any money. We were a family company whose philosophy was all about making a profit. Why wear out our equipment here for peanuts when there were operators willing to pay top rates in other Middle Eastern countries?

I was spending five days a week in a short-term furnished rental apartment in Abu Dhabi and staying the weekend in one of Frank's staff apartments in Dubai. One Thursday evening, I was driving back to Dubai at about 100 miles an hour. I was tired and it had been a very long, hot day. The sun was just about to go down and I wanted to get back before it was dark. All of a sudden, right in front of me on the highway were camels. I stood on the brakes and the car started to skid from side to side. I was laying rubber down all over the road and my door mirror slammed against the door as it hit one of the camel's legs. The car came to an abrupt halt on the side of the road, some 20 yards past the camels, who was still standing in the middle of the fucking road! Camels are not the smartest animals but they spat at me as I finally drove past. Back in Dubai – and after a few drinks at the Red Lion – my heart rate was back to normal.

Ellie was due to visit the following weekend and I had made an effort to lose some weight. Early every morning, I went jogging with Dick around Safa Park. I managed 2km, at which point Dick would take off like a flash to complete a further 5km. I had managed to lose a few pounds but I needed to brighten up my appearance. I decided to get a perm and blond streaks in my hair. I felt like a proper prat as I sat in a chair in a ladies' hair salon for a couple of hours with a hundred strips of aluminium foil in my hair – and the smell was something else!

I stood outside the arrivals hall in red shoes, blue jeans, a Hawaiian shirt and with my new hairstyle – and Ellie walked straight past me! I had to run after her. I called out her name and she stopped and looked at me. Then she smiled. "Don't tell me you've also bought a Harley-Davidson!" she said.

The JPO contract was running well and I was only weeks away from my month back home. By this time, Keith seemed to live on a plane as he was constantly flying around the world – Far East, Middle East, Europe – but he had come to Dubai on a visit. Dick was in Oman for a few days so it was up to me to entertain Keith. During one of our lunches together, Keith asked me about working in Aberdeen and the North Sea. He said he was interested in opening a small base there. So I told him that Weatherford and Salvesen Casing Crews both had big operations in Aberdeen, with both companies having over 40 technicians plus office staff and workshops.

There was a long history of these two companies cutting each other's throats to pick up the big Shell, BP and Mobil contracts and I said: "Keith, if you open in

Aberdeen you have to think big for any of the operators to take you seriously."

The day before I left for my vacation, I was sitting by the pool at the staff apartment when Dick turned up. "While you're back in Aberdeen, Maxi Gremillion will be there and he wants to talk to you," he said.

"About what?" I asked.

"Frank's is opening a base in Aberdeen and he would like to have some input from you before you return to Dubai."

I wasn't home two days before Maxi Gremillion phoned me. "Hey, Les, can we meet for lunch today at the Earl's Court Hotel?" During lunch, Maxi told me he was moving his family to Aberdeen from Houston to set up Frank's International UK. This was the first time I had heard the name and he handed me one of his cards, which said 'VP, Frank's International UK'. I was told equipment was on the water and would arrive within three weeks and that Frank's had a small office and workshop at Alexander House in Altens and he wanted me to be the new operations manager. I knew Ellie wouldn't move back to the Middle East so, after settling the terms of my new contract, I told Maxi I would take the job – but that he had to tell Dick I wasn't coming back to Dubai.

The next day I got a call from Dick, telling me he hoped the new job went well and that he would see me in September at the Aberdeen Oil Show.

Frank's International UK, 1997

Frank's International UK got off to a slow start, with problems from one of the offshore government agencies blocking the start-up. Frank's had been in business since 1938 and was the largest supplier of TRS services and pipe sales in the States – and one or more of our competitors had complained that we were a predatory company and would drive prices down. While all this was being sorted out legally, Frank's was helped out by a company they had been in talks with about supporting some of their oilfield equipment internationally, so they began trading under the name Howden Frank's. This partnership was only going to be temporary until the legal problem was sorted out.

Our first job in the North Sea was on 23rd August for Exxon/Mobil on Rig DF-93, running a string of 9⅝" casing, and it was a great success. The legal problem was eventually solved and Frank's International UK was in business. Frank's went from strength to strength, opening an office and workshop in Great Yarmouth to service the southern North Sea and to house the hammer department. Frank's was one of the biggest conductor pipe hammer companies in the world and over the next few years they would purchase three UK hammer companies based in Great Yarmouth. Maxi was based in Aberdeen as VP and an old friend of mine, Andy Jenner was the UK manager, based in Great Yarmouth.

Within 12 months, Frank's had been awarded a

bigger, longer term contract with Marathon Oil, which would be the foundation for the company moving forward. A larger office and workshop complex were purchased just around the corner from Alexander House. That first year, the company ran lean and mean, saving money where it could. I would collect the technicians from their homes and run them to the heliport in Dyce in my own car; this meant I was working seven days a week. As the company grew in size and the number of technicians grew, a taxi company took over, which gave me more time to take care of the day to day equipment load outs and roster of 35 technicians who were now based out of Aberdeen. This wasn't difficult, as I put procedures in place and there wasn't a lot of paperwork involved.

The next couple of years were very messy for me, both personally and business-wise. Ellie had informed me she didn't love me and she wanted a divorce. The divorce was all sorted out within a couple of months; it was very quick as there were no children involved. The lower west wing of Tillycorthie Mansion House sold very quickly, and our savings, cars, furniture and valuables were split 50/50. I moved into a new bungalow in Queens Den, just off North Anderson. Ellie soon married Mark, a work colleague, and she gave birth to the baby girl she had been longing for.

I needed to move on and I wasn't in a hurry to get my heart broken for a third time. I put all my spare time into AVN, the video company I set up before going back to Dubai. I liked making films. I headhunted a young guy from one of the established video companies in

Aberdeen and offered him a partnership in the company. Duncan Malcolm would run the day to day business and I would look after the finances.

There was always a good laugh to be had on Fridays after a long week in the office. Many of the oilfield managers met up in the Egg and Dart bar at the Earl's Court Hotel. The place was always full and the hotel owner, George, would hand out free fish and chips wrapped in newspaper. Maxi would be there telling funny stories that used to crack me up and there were always lots of good-looking women there to brighten up the place. My new house was only a 5-minute walk from the Egg and Dart and should I drink over the driving limit, I would retrieve my car the next morning.

I remember one night, Maxi was in the middle of a long joke about a super salesman and one of his shooting mates when Barry came up to him and said: "Your car's on fire!"

Maxi looked at him and said, "Yeah, right."

The next thing you know, there were fire engine sirens and flashes of blue lights coming through the bar windows. We all rushed outside to see two fire tenders spraying foam all over a Vauxhall estate in the car park, and Maxi shouting out, "Oh no, that's my wife's car!" Maxi later found out that the petrol pipe from the tank to the carburettor had leaked onto the hot exhaust pipe. On the plus side, his wife got a new car, so I guess she had the last laugh.

Business at Frank's was going from strength to strength. We had taken on a new sales manager, my old boss from Weatherford Indonesia, Jim Sayer. Small world. It wasn't long after that that Maxi and his family returned to the Houston head office and he was promoted to VP, International Operations. During 1988, Mr Frank passed away and Donald Mosing became president of the company and Keith CEO. There were other moves in Aberdeen: Jim was made the manager and John Walker was made up to sales manager.

As for me, my life was getting messy. I was focusing too much of my time on AVN – and it showed. One day, Keith phoned me and asked if AVN could make a film about the history of Frank's, as the company had just celebrated 50 years in business. Before I knew it, I was on a plane to Houston with AVN's new broadcast camera and sound kit and lots of recording cassettes. I had met Donald Mosing during his visits to Aberdeen, but on this trip I got to meet all the Mosing family, including Miss Jessie, Mr Frank's wife, and I recorded their stories. AVN went on to make a second film for Frank's.

I was sticking my neck out and asking to get my head cut off – and it was. I was called into Jim's office and handed an envelope. The serious look on his face told me this was not good news. Inside was a letter and a cheque for £7,000. I looked at the letter but all I could see were rows of words jumping around the page.

Jim broke the silence. "I am sorry, Les. We had to make your position redundant."

I knew I had fucked up. AVN was in the red and bleeding me dry. I could have told Jim that my job wasn't redundant, they were just changing the role name and promoting my service supervisor John Lethbridge into my position. I could have taken legal action for unfair dismissal. But I decided there and then to try and make a go of running AVN. So I signed the letter and took the money. I didn't want to burn all my bridges with Frank's. If things didn't work out, I might have to return to the company in the future.

AVN Ltd., 1993

Over the next 12 months, it was a struggle to make enough money to pay wages and studio costs. We had a great deal sub-renting a prestigious West End office suite on Rubislaw Terrace, off Albyn Place; it was a good location to promote the company and be taken seriously. We made safety induction videos for Frank's, Shell, Conoco, Noble Drilling and some manufacturing companies as far away as Glasgow. We also made 30- and 60-second adverts for television and we produced the first advert promoting a funeral director to be shown on national TV. But the money was going out faster than it was coming in.

At the beginning of 1994, I phoned Keith Mosing in Houston. I was put straight through to him. He asked how I was and was interested to find out how AVN was doing. I told him I was losing my ass and going deeper into debt every month – and I needed a job. Keith told me he would look out for something and get back to me ASAP.

One week later, I got a call from Keith Vuillemont, the regional manager for West Africa. I remembered Keith from the Houston office when I was in the States making the video *50 Golden Years*; he was now based in Pau, France, which was the regional office for West Africa as most of his clients there were French-speaking and Keith spoke Cajun French.

"Les," he said, "Keith Mosing ask me to contact you

and offer you a manager's position in Nigeria." Now, I had always been told never to work in Nigeria. There was a long silence from my end. Keith quickly said: "It's a rotational job, Les. Two managers working six weeks on and four weeks off."

Now this I knew I could do, so I said yes, and so began the rest of my working life, with Frank's in the oilfield. Duncan carried on running AVN and I would keep pumping money into the company and working in the office on my four weeks off.

During 1994, we made a film about malt whisky. The film was a big production, costing over £56,000 when you took into account studio time, script writers, narration, original music scores, vocals, actors and the hire of a helicopter for several days. The film was about the Malt Whisky Trail in Speyside, the history and manufacture of whisky and visits to the eight single malt distilleries on the trail, finding out about the families that started these companies. I did my research and found out that over 450,000 people visited the trail during 1993. The eight distilleries were happy to permit us to make the film and gave us all the help we needed during filming. The film received great reviews from people who purchased a copy but was a financial flop, making only £5,000 to date. This was because after the film was finished the eight distilleries decided not to sell the video in their whisky shops, putting a stop to over 450,000 potential sales each year. Apparently, they felt they would be advertising their competitors' whisky! This was a blow, because we'd thought we would make our fortune. We were left trying to sell the video through shops at £12.99 per copy; by the time the shop and distributor and video duplication company had taken their bit, we were left with £2.50 a copy, less VAT.

The start of 1998 saw the introduction of very expensive superior digital studio equipment, and we could see the writing on the wall for AVN. The new digital technology would make analogue studio equipment redundant in the very near future and we didn't have the money to make the switch. Duncan was headhunted by a big production company in Edinburgh and was keen to move on. It was time to put AVN to bed.

Frank's Nigeria, 1994-1999

I needed to apply for a Nigerian work visa and I screwed up the paperwork by not filling out the form correctly. I sent in a second form to the Nigerian Embassy. After seven days, I hadn't heard anything back from them and I started to get worried. I should have asked Frank's in Aberdeen for help but I didn't want them to have anything to do with my new job. I phoned the embassy when they opened and was put through to the visa department. They told me my application was under review because of the first form not complying with the minimum requirements, and they would get back to me ASAP.

My next call was to my brother David, who was high up in the immigration department at Globe House in London. I told Dave my problem and asked if he knew anyone in the Nigerian Embassy that could help me get my work visa sorted out. Dave told me he would make some calls but that it would cost him in the future as that was how things were done in diplomatic circles. Within the hour, I received a call from the Nigerian Embassy informing me that my work visa would be ready for collection at 10 o'clock the next morning.

I booked a ticket to Lagos for the next day and packed my bag. I arrived at the Nigerian Embassy about 10 am and picked up my passport, which now had a full page showing my Nigerian work visa. Then there was a mad dash on two trains to get across London for my British

Airways flight from Heathrow to Lagos.

I ran to the desk, knowing they were already boarding the plane. The girl at the desk said, "I was just going to close the flight. You will have to run to the gate before they close the door. I'll phone them and tell them you are coming but you have to be quick!" Then she added, "And I'm not sure your suitcase will make the flight!"

They were waiting for me at the gate and as I walked through the door of the plane, everyone was already seated. I got the feeling they were thinking, "Who the fuck is he?" I was shown to a window seat in the first row of economy and as I sat down, the jumbo jet was being pushed back.

I slept most of the way, only to be woken up when they started serving breakfast. It was very early in the morning when we touched down in Lagos. The doors opened and I was one of the first to disembark, after business and first-class passengers. I followed the people in front of me, who seemed to know where they were going. At the end of the walkway, they took the escalator up and at the top of the escalator were two soldiers holding machine guns.

I followed everyone into a room. Laid out on tables was a full breakfast buffet, and glasses of champagne were being handed out by waiters. I took another look at my fellow passengers and noticed they were all wearing identity badges with their name on and 'British Embassy' underneath. I had followed a business delegation and I needed to get out of the room as fast as I could!

Once outside, I looked down to see the rest of the passengers taking the escalator down to passport control. So now I was the last person to go through passport control and immigration and currency control. It was like running the gauntlet but being last meant I got through without any hassle; I think they just wanted to finish their night shift and go home. I was pretty sure my suitcase wouldn't have made the flight but there it was, waiting for me on the carousel.

I walked straight through customs and made my way out to the arrivals hall, where I was met by two Nigerian guys hold a sign with my name on it. They told me they were from the car hire company that Frank's used in Lagos. Suddenly, the whole airport was plunged into darkness – you couldn't see your hand in front of your face. One of the guys said, "Hold onto your bags, sir, and don't let go." I could hear generators kicking in and then the lights came back on.

We drove through Lagos to the internal airport, where I was met by Felix, the owner of the car hire company, who welcomed me to Nigeria. The place was full of people buying tickets to locations around the country. It was like a zoo; you were bombarded with "Can I carry your bags?" and "Do you want to buy this?" and kids asking for money. Felix appeared from one of the ticket desks with my ticket to Port Harcourt. We pushed our way through the crowd and into the departure terminal. The flight was on an old Soviet Aeroflot reject, which concerned me, but it got me to my destination in about an hour. Port Harcourt airport was also a zoo, but smaller.

A Frank's driver drove me straight to the staff house and I walked into the dining room to be greeted by six expatriate technicians and my French back-to-back manager, Mitchell Dashain, who were all having lunch. It wasn't hard settling in – I never had that problem – but having a week's handover was hard work. We both had different ideas about the day to day running of the company, so Mitchell and I decided to start working five weeks on and five weeks off. This didn't cost the company any more money and Keith endorsed it. This was a much better deal – more time off and we only needed a couple of hours to hand over – but there was a downside to this, which was that I would walk in to a pile of shit that Mitchell should have closed out but hadn't, leaving them for me to deal with.

Mitchell and I worked back to back for the next six years and there are a lot of stories to tell you about my time in Nigeria. The first year we were working under WASCO, who were our Nigerian agent; they had a lot of warehouses and offices and the arrangement suited Frank's. On one of my first trips I had a radio call on my handset; nothing worked in Port Harcourt: no phones, no electricity except for our big generators. It was Wally Black, telling me to stay in my office as there was a problem with some of his sub-contractors out in the yard. I could hear a lot of shouting and screaming, so I made my way to reception and looked through the window to see six men standing over another man who was on his knees with a metal bucket over his head. They were hitting him over the head with big sticks.

I said to the secretary, "What's the problem?"

"They think he's a thief," she replied.

These guys were employed to move cement sacks from trucks into the warehouses. It was a tough job and they only wore loincloths and flip flops. They were all muscle; I remembered seeing them the week before, showering naked underneath the warehouse tin roof during a rain storm, and they were hung like donkeys. I thought to myself, *These guys couldn't have had any toys when they were kids*! There was no way you would have got me to shower next them; I mean, I grew up with lots of toys. Anyway, the locals had their own way of settling scores, whether it was one on one or village against village – and you got involved at your peril.

I have picked out a few classic stories from my time in Nigeria, so here we go.

The Ogoni Nine

I awoke on 10th October 1995 to the sound of someone calling us on the VHF radio in the living room. It was the radio operator from Mobil Six. I pressed the button on the handset and said: Mobil six Frank's Hotel, over." I thought he was going to ask for a crew to go out to one of their rigs to run casing. But no, he told me that Port Harcourt was under a curfew and no one was allowed out of the compound. All the roads had been blocked, the army were on the streets and there were armoured tanks in place. I let the other technicians know what was going on, but at this stage I didn't know what the problem was.

After breakfast, I walked out of the staff house to talk to one of the compound security guards. He told me that, earlier that morning, the government had hung the Ogoni Nine in Port Harcourt. The Ogoni Nine were a group of activists that included Ken Saro-Wiwa, a Nigerian writer, television producer, environmentalist and winner of the Right Livelihood Award and the Goldman Environmental Prize. Saro-Wiwa was a member of the Ogoni people, an ethnic minority in Nigeria whose homeland, Ogoniland, was in the Niger delta area and had been targeted for crude oil extraction since the 1950s. He led an activist campaign against oil pollution in his homeland and was tried by a special military tribune for allegedly masterminding the gruesome murder of an Ogoni chief at a pro-government meeting. Saro-Wiwa was sentenced to hang in 1995 by the military dictatorship of General Sani Abacha. His execution provoked international outrage and Nigeria was suspension from the Commonwealth of Nations for over three years.

The next day, life in Port Harcourt return to normal, with the army and police lifting the curfew and dismantling the roadblocks. You just didn't know what tomorrow would bring when working in Nigeria.

Bunny Hops and Swimming Lessons

This is a rare funny Nigerian story... That is, it's funny if you're not Yudi.

We had finished work for the day. The first car left for the five-minute drive from the base to the staff house compound in Trans Amadia, and my car left about five minutes later. We turned right at the junction and were about to take a quick left through the compound gates when my driver Edit said: "Look sir, it's Yudi! He's been stopped by the police at the junction." I looked back and could see our four technicians standing outside their car. The police had Yudi at gunpoint and they were making him jump up and down like a rabbit. "He's bunny hopping!" Edit said. It looked like the whole village was at the event. The police started shouting at Yudi and he began to mimic doing the breaststroke in a muddy pool of water in front of the car.

By now the doors of our compound had opened and we had to move on as there was another car behind us, also waiting to enter the compound. About 15 minutes later, Yudi delivered the technicians safely back. The guys all came into the staff house and said that the police had let Yudi go after they had given the cops some small change for soft drinks. Apparently, the police had pulled them over and Yudi had decided to be a bit mouthy with them, so they pulled him out of the car at gun point and made him do bunny hops and swim to teach him a lesson...

A Riot of a Time

Normally, during my five-week tour in Nigeria I would make one or two visits to Lagos. This meant taking a flight down to the city and spending two days visiting clients. The main objectives were to pick up payment cheques in nairas for invoices and visit drilling superintendents and drilling managers to make sure there were no problems I didn't know about with our service and resolve any outstanding issues.

So, my day began with a drive to Port Harcourt airport to catch a flight. Everything seemed normal – well, I don't think it was ever normal, but by now I had been working in Nigeria for some years and I was used to running the gauntlet through the crowded hallways of the airport, solving problems with security and airline bureaucracy. It takes about an hour to fly to Lagos and you know that any problems at this end are going to be even worse when you land. On this occasion, though, the local airport was very quiet; no one tried to carry my bags or sell me something, no pushing or shoving. You always kept a firm grip on your bag and your valuables, just in case they tried to steal from you.

I could see my driver waiting for me; I knew him pretty well by now. Today he was going to drive me across Lagos and over to Victoria Island. "Why is it so quiet?" I asked him.

He told me the union members were rioting all over the city, because General Sani Abacha, the Nigerian

President, had jailed the labour union's leaders. "I don't think it is a good idea to drive to Victoria Island today, sir," he said.

I said, "Well, let's see how bad it is." I had set up several meetings with clients from Port Harcourt, which was not easy to do because of the poor communications in the country.

We drove away from the local airport and at first it didn't seem too bad – but this was to change as soon as we got to the expressway. We saw people being chased by police and soldiers. Cars were coming the wrong way down the expressway, flashing their headlights and sounding their horns.

My driver said, "Sir, I think we should turn back."

I thought for a minute and said: "No, keep driving."

We were having to dodge cars left and right; there were burning tyres on the road and people standing on the viaducts, throwing rocks down at the passing cars. I could see from the face of my driver that he was getting quite scared and I was starting to think maybe we should have turned back when he said. But I was convinced that when we reached the causeway, things would quieten down.

We reached the causeway, where we were stopped by a police roadblock. Once they saw there was an expat in the car they waved us through. The streets were empty as we entered Victoria Island, and before long we were outside the Chevron Oil office complex. I showed my ID card to security but they told me the office was closed for the day, because of the trouble in Lagos; they were worried it could spill over onto the island.

We drove next to Mobil Oil, where we were told the same thing by their security guards. So, with nothing else to do, I gave my driver money to find some accommodation and I booked myself into the Radisson Hotel.

The next day, the oil company offices were open and I did my business. I left the island the following day and the drive back to Lagos was uneventful. There were still rocks and burned tyres by the side of the road but people were back on the streets, going about their lives.

The local airport was also back to being a zoo – but that was just normal.

Rough Justice

The traffic in Port Harcourt could be very busy at certain times of the day. In the dry season, we could take a shortcut through one of the villages to get back to the workshop. In the wet season this was not possible, because the roads were made of mud and you stood a big chance of getting stuck.

This particular afternoon, we were driving through the village when we had to slow down for two policemen. They were carrying guns and marching three Nigerian men down the road: naked men who were bleeding from their mouths, noses and various other parts of their bodies. One of the men was carrying a car battery, one held a car headlamp and the other a car number plate.

"They are car thieves," my driver said.

"Where are they going?" I asked.

"The police are taking them to the Trans Amadi police station." This was the first time I had seen naked men being marched through Trans Amadi, and we said no more about it.

The next day, driving over to Mobil six we passed the Trans Amadi police station, which stood near the main road and was surrounded by about an acre of land. There were three tall white flagpoles outside the main door and there, still covered in blood and handcuffed to the poles with their feet shackled in chains, were the three naked Nigerian men we'd seen yesterday.

I asked my driver, Eddit: "What's happening here?"

"The word is that they will be executed later today," he said.

"For stealing car parts?!"

"I don't really know."

"Will they hang them?" I asked.

"No, no," he replied. "They'll take them into the jungle and have them dig their own graves. Then they'll stand them in the hole and shoot them in the head."

Now guys, I wasn't there, so I can't verify this. But the Nigerian police were renowned for their rough justice.

Nailed

If you ask anyone who has worked in Nigeria for any length of time whether they ever saw a dead body on the street, the answer will be yes – unless they were blind. Life in Nigeria can be pretty cheap, especially if you are caught stealing from other Nigerians, and Nigerian onlookers will not report a dead body to the police as it might implicate them in the killing.

This true story is not for the faint-hearted. It all started early one morning. We drove out of the staff house compound and down through Trans Amadi industrial estate, passing the slaughterhouse and the large Halliburton base. We were just approaching the small railway bridge when we spotted the body of a man lying in the middle of the road. We had to slow down to avoid running over him. This was a very busy road, with lots of cars and trucks, and people walking past the dead man, going to work and to the various food markets. I could even see children carrying buckets of water on their heads; they collected the water from the local well because there was no water supply in their houses.

I looked down at the dead man and said to Eddit: "There's a six-inch nail sticking out of the top of his head!"

Eddit said, "Yes, he must be a thief and was caught by some villagers who killed him."

It was quite disturbing knowing that the local Trans Amadi police station was just half a kilometre down the road. I said to Eddit: "We should stop and tell the police there's a dead body on the road."

"No, sir!" Eddit said. "We can't get involved. That's a very dangerous idea." So we drove on.

Later that day, we were going back to the staff house and we again passed the body. It was midday and very hot – and the body was all bloated up. The next morning we passed the dead man again. This time he was naked: someone had taken his shoes and his clothing during the night. He had been run over by several vehicles and was a right mess. He was still in the middle of the road when I returned from my meeting. Two men were picking up body parts and shovelling what was left of him into a rubbish truck.

During the time I worked in Nigeria I saw a lot of bodies, but this one was shocking.

The Nigerian Dentist

Shortly before a trip to Nigeria, one of my fillings fell out. I went to my local dentist and was told I would need a root canal but they couldn't do it for 10 days. So I told them I would call them when I got back in five weeks' time.

I arrived back in Nigeria on a Friday night. We normally had what we called safety meetings on Fridays, though they were really a social gathering of all the service companies at the Elf Aquitaine staff house bar. Frank's would supply the pizzas, everyone else would bring drinks and we all had a good time telling tales and have a laugh, away from the hustle and bustle of life in Port Harcourt.

I mentioned to one of the guys at the bar that I had a problem with my tooth and he said: "Well, why don't you get it fixed here?"

"What, in Nigeria?" I said. "Are you crazy?"

"There's a very good dentist in Trans Amadi," he replied. "His name is Chief Green. He trained in America and has the latest equipment and a very clean surgery."

So, the next morning I went down to see Chief Green. He sat me down and looked at my tooth. Then he said: "Yes, you're going to need a root canal," and he started sketching out exactly what he would have to do. I must say, I've never had a dentist sketch out a procedure for me before, and I thought this was pretty good. He told me he could fit me in the next day at 10 o'clock, so the next morning I arrived at his surgery and he started the procedure. Everything was going fine until we suddenly lost all power; the Nigerian electric company was absolute useless and you could never tell when the power was going to cut out. In fact, it could be out for a day or six months; that's why every company had their own generator.

Chief Green said to me, "Listen, I'll go down to my generator and start it up. It'll only take five minutes."

So I'm sitting in the chair, hoping it won't take any longer than five minutes because the injection might start to wear off and I'm not one for pain. Five minutes later, the lights came on, the air conditioning started working and Chief Green reappeared and started drilling away inside my tooth.

All of a sudden, he stopped. "Oh," he said. "We have a problem. The suction machine is not working because we don't have enough power to run all the machinery. Never mind, we'll carry on. My nurse will just have to keep changing the dressings around your tooth because we need to soak up the saliva. We don't want it getting into the cavity or you'll get an infection." So, for the next 15 minutes, the nurse kept renewing the wadding. Chief Green finished the procedure and I thanked him and paid my bill.

This was 26 years ago and I have not had any problems with that tooth since.

Blood on the Ground

Here is a story about an incident I will always remember.

We had recently moved from our old base to a new larger complex in Trans Amadi. The old base was next to a village, let's called it Village A, from where we employed all our staff. I normally visited clients first thing each morning and on this particular day, I got a call from the base supervisor, telling me I should return to the base as soon as possible, as there were over 80 villagers protesting outside the gates. When I arrived at the base, I found out the villagers were very upset that we hadn't hired anyone from their village to work on the base. Unbeknown to us, the new base was between two villages – Village A and Village B – and the people living in Village B were very angry that all our staff came from Village A!

I managed to slip my way through the crowd and entered the base through the side door. Two mobile police officers were standing near the office door and as I entered, I could hear a lot of shouting. My staff had let four of the crowd into the base to hear their demands but this had escalated into a big argument. Margaret, one of my office secretaries, had taken off her high-heeled shoe and hit one of them on the side of the head and he was bleeding.

I managed to cool things down and asked the four villagers to come into my office. I listened to their demands and told them I would discuss it with my regional manager and find out how many new employees we could hire from their village. I asked them to come back to see me at the end of the week. They left and the crowd dispersed.

I was then approached by Felix, one of our purchasing agents, who said I would need assistance from the king of Port Harcourt to resolve this issue, as there had been blood spilled.

Later that day, our mobile police officer told me the gates had been sealed up by the local juju man (witch doctor) and none of our Nigerian staff or truck drivers would enter the base. In other words, no equipment could come in or go out and we needed equipment available and ready to be sent out to the rigs to run casing! This was a real problem.

The next morning, I had a visit from the prince of Port Harcourt. He was a well-dressed man who talked like an English public-school boy; someone told me he had been educated in the UK. He told me that the fact that blood had been spilled was very serious and he outlined what had to be done.

One: We would have to employ people from Village B.

Two: Prayers would need to be chanted by the juju man at the four corners of Port Harcourt and then the juju man would open the gates.

Three: We would have to hold a party in each village and purchase two cows for each banquet.

Four: I would have to attend a meeting with the king and the village elders and say that I was sorry for blood being spilled.

We ended up hiring five new staff, mostly cleaners and yard labourers, and Felix looked after the purchase of the cows and the rest of the food and drinks for the parties. When I arrived at the king's compound, I was given a chief's hat, tunic and trousers and a brass-headed ebony walking stick. The king made me an honorary Chief of Port Harcourt, I made my apologies to the elders and I think everyone had a good time at their parties.

Things went back to normal at the base and I was happy that this had been all sorted out – even though I knew it was a case of extortion.

My 419 Christmas

So here I am, celebrating my fourth – but not my final – Christmas in Nigeria. This is what happens if you have no kids: your back-to-back says you should work Christmas and have New Year off so he can spend the festive season with his daughter. Anyway, it suited me to have New Year off.

We only had a small workforce and as I was the one working Christmas, it was always my responsibility to make sure the local employees received their Christmas bonus on Christmas Eve. If it had been money, this would've been pretty painless – but no, they wanted to be given a gallon of cooking oil, a 25kg bag of basmati rice and a live chicken.

For the first three years, I perfected this process. I made sure it was the right type of oil and that the bag of rice did weigh 25kg and not 19kg, but especially that the chickens were all alive and kicking. No Nigerian wants a dead chicken; there's no electricity at home for a fridge.

But this year, we had a problem. Since the company had moved into larger premises and taken on more employees, it had put us on the radar of all the government agencies, who were expecting Christmas presents from Frank's. During the week leading up to Christmas, there was a daily stream of agency reps visiting me and reminding me that they had been working throughout the year on our behalf, and that the government had not paid their salaries for several months, and because of that, their children and family would suffer through Christmas. Most of them I recognised, and they would turn up wearing their uniforms: customs, army, air force, police and, of course, the immigration department.

So this year I was sitting at my desk, around 4 pm on 23rd December, when my accountant came into my office with two Nigerians who I hadn't seen before. They presented themselves as immigration officers and said their boss was in town for the annual regional immigration controllers meeting; he would like to see me at the Presidential Hotel and they had come to take me to him. Now, anyone who has worked in Nigeria will know the expression 'Four, nineteen', after section four, clause nineteen of the Nigerian penal code, which relates to fraudulent schemes. And I had those number, 4-19, flashing in front of my eyes right now. I came up with a quick excuse and said they had not given me enough time and I had a meeting planned with a client, so I would not be able to go with them. They were a little peeved at this and said their boss would not like the fact that he had been snubbed. Anyway, they left my office, never to return – I hoped.

Well, that hope was quickly crushed on Christmas Eve morning, when a Jeep arrived carrying six men in military uniforms and carrying AK-47 machine guns! The two men who had been in my office the previous afternoon were again standing in front of my desk, now in uniform and with their medals and rank in full view. They told me their boss was waiting to see me in his hotel room and that he was not happy. "If you don't come along right now," one of them said, "we will arrest you as an illegal alien."

So I asked my accountant to fetch my driver and told the two messengers that I would meet them at the hotel. Well, one of them got right up in my face and said, "Get in our truck. You travel with us." Obviously, I told my driver to follow them.

We arrived at the Presidential Hotel and I was marched up to an executive suite, along with my accountant. We were told to wait for the immigration controller, as he was taking a shower. Fifteen minutes later, the bedroom door – which had armed guards standing either side of it – opened and out came a short guy in a string vest and boxer shorts. Everyone in the room jumped to attention. He looked at me and said, "So you were too busy to see me yesterday?"

"One has to be careful who one drives off with in Port Harcourt," I replied, "and as these men had turned up with no official uniforms or identity cards, I thought this was a case of a 419."

"They are undercover agents," he said, and he told me to wait while he got changed. Another 20 minutes passed before he returned from his bedroom, this time in full uniform, his chest full of medals and gold braid on his shoulders. "Let's go," he said.

"Where?" was my reply.

"I'm too busy to talk to you here in Port Harcourt so I am taking you to my office in Eket."

At this point, my accountant stepped forward and said, "Can I have a minute with your officers?" I was told to sit down again and the immigration controller left the room, saying he would wait for me in his car.

By now I knew lots of my workers would be waiting for their chickens back at base, but it was looking like I could be spending Christmas in a jail cell, some three and half hours' drive away. Of course, I knew this was all a game, but it was up to me to write the final chapter in the story.

My accountant and the two officers came back and sat next to me and it was all laid out. To avoid going to Eket, I needed to pay homage to appease my host. I asked him what he would like for Christmas. "Oh, not much," was the answer. "Just a basket with chocolates and biscuits and a bottle of Johnny Walker black label whisky and 4,000 naira in cash." (About $100.) This being Christmas Eve, I really didn't want to be stuck in a cell for the festive season, or at best spend seven hours in a car to and from Eket. Plus, we had been having some immigration problems lately at the heliport with our expat crew and I was told this would be all solved. So the deal was done.

One month later, I had a phone call from the controller, thanking me for the whisky. Three months later, the company fired the accountant for theft. It makes you think: was this a double case of 419, with the accountant setting up the whole thing and splitting the money with the two officers? Or is that just me being paranoid?

A good tip for anyone going to work in Nigeria: you will be asked in airports, "What have you got for me?" and the answer should always be, "My blessing on you and your family." Trust me, this works. It's all in the eyes; their ability to smell fresh meat is astonishing. So smile and stay calm at all times.

The Nigerian Accountant

I drove through the office gates one lovely sunny morning. The base was only a stone's throw away from Port Harcourt slaughter market, and the vultures were all lined up along the roof, looking down at my office staff and workshop technicians, who were standing around in the car park. The first thing that jumped into my head was: "Fuck! They've all gone on strike!" But no, I was told that we'd been robbed and the security guard had been found out the back of the warehouse, gagged and tied up and smelling of shit.

I entered the office, which had been trashed: tables and chairs were upside down and our safe had been opened with the aid of a sledgehammer. Expat passports thrown all over the floor; one of them had been torn up. We had purchased the safe locally some months earlier. Lumps of filler – the stuff you use to repair damaged areas on a car – had broken off it; it was obvious it had been broken into before, repaired, painted and sold to us as new. Fortunately there hadn't been any petty cash left in the safe the night before as it had been taken back to the staff house to pay for water and diesel. So, the thieves had ended up stealing an American passport, the fax copying machine and the company communications equipment – UHF and VHF radios.

We phoned the police and later that morning the local CID arrived on the crime scene. They told us they needed a photographer, the loan of a car and a driver, and some money for food, Coca Cola and Sprite before they could start the investigation and apprehend the criminals. The officers took advantage of the car for the rest of the week without coming up with a single thing, so we decided to drop the case and get back to a normal working life – or as normal as you can in Nigeria.

Some weeks later, some of the stolen equipment appeared for sale in the Port Harcourt market. Word on the street was that our accountant had mastermind the robbery. We had had our eyes on this employee for some months and this was the last straw. He was confronted and didn't deny the theft; he just said nothing. He was dismissed on the spot.

The following Friday, at 4 pm, I was driving back from visiting a client when I got a call on the radio from the base supervisor, telling me not to return to the office as there were two CID officers waiting to arrest me. Now, from my experience over the years, I knew that if you were going to be arrested or served a summons, it always happened on a Friday, late afternoon. You may ask why… Well, it's all down to intimidation. At that time of the day, you'd have no access to your lawyer over the weekend and they knew you wouldn't want to be locked up in a police cell until Monday morning.

I told my supervisor that I would go right away to my lawyer's office before she closed for the weekend, but I was outsmarted by my ex-accountant, who had thought about this and was scanning my radio calls – ironically, probably on a VHS radio he stole from our office.

It took an age to get across town because of the bad traffic. Suddenly, a car came from nowhere and ran us to the side of the road. The two CID officers and the accountant jumped out of the car. The officers quickly flashed their warrant cards and told me to get out of my car and into the accountant's. So I did, but not before telling my driver to follow us; you always need someone to know where you are being detained.

Once I was in the car, the three men presented me with an arrest warrant. I looked at it and all I could see were lines of text that made no sense. Eventually, I calmed down and could see it stated that I had been accused of unfairly dismissing the accountant and I needed to give up my passport to the court or I would be detained. The police had told the judge they feared I would skip the country unless the court held my passport until the case came to court.

I told them my passport was at the staff house and we would need to go there first. We arrived and I gave them my passport and was then told they would keep me in a police cell until Monday as new charges were going to be filed against me for spying! Well, spying. I know, all bullshit. I needed to stop this and I knew what to do, so I asked the two officers if I could have a private chat with them. Some small amount of money was paid and they left the house with my passport – but left me in the house.

Monday morning, I saw my lawyer. She checked with the court and told me my passport was being held by them. There was no word when my case would be heard and I was advised to get a second passport from the British High Commission in Lagos, which I did. I knew Mitchell would be returning from leave the following week and I needed to do something, so I talked to my lawyer and she said she would have a word with her uncle, who was a judge in Port Harcourt, and see what he could do.

When I told Mitchell what had happened, he said: "I think you will have to use your new passport and leave."

I hated being held over a barrel by the accountant; it made my blood boil. If I was to leave on my second passport, there would be no returning to Nigeria and I would lose my job. So I said to Mitchell, "No, I am not leaving."

After lunch the next day, my lawyer turned up at the office waving my passport in the air. "You can go now, I got the charges dropped!" she shouted. Mitchell looked as happy as I did; he wanted me out of the way so he could start running the company his way. Back at the house, I packed my bag and got into the car to go to the airport. My lawyer came with me to make sure there were no problems.

We arrived at the airport and there at the ticket office was the accountant and his girlfriend, purchasing a ticket to Lagos! He saw me, our eyes made contact and he moved away into the departure lounge and out of sight. Eventually, after a mad rush and paying over the odds for a ticket, I was led through a side door and pushed out by my lawyer onto the tarmac apron. The plane's engines were starting to get louder and louder and I could see a stewardess waving at me from the door of the plane. I started to speed up and heard footsteps coming from behind me. It was my lawyer with my suitcase, which I had forgotten! I took hold of the bag, gave her a big hug and thanked her for everything. Then I ran up the stairs and into the plane, just as the door was closed behind me. The plane was not the normal type you would take to Lagos; it was a big 272 aircraft but it only had eight seats – and two of them were taken up by a very nervous accountant and his girlfriend!

By now, you're probably thinking this is all a bit far-fetched. I mean, it seemed that way to me too. Like a black and white movie unfolding, I could see the trailer to the film. Man escaping the country, woman in tears running down the runway behind him, both stooping to embrace, the plane ready to take off at any moment, man reaching the door to the plane, door closing behind him... OK, OK, back to the story.

I sat down in my seat just as the aircraft started to scream down the runway. I looked around the aircraft. The other five seats were taken up by businessmen wearing pinstripes. I loved the look on the accountant's sweaty face. During the flight, I started to wonder why the accountant was on the same plane as me, along with five guys who looked like lawyers. Just because you're paranoid, it doesn't mean they are not out to get you! The flight normally takes about an hour to Lagos and I hadn't been given a boarding card, so I started wondering if I was even going to Lagos! So now I was the one starting to sweat. But then the penny dropped. No – *he's* the one who is escaping! He must have heard that my charges had been dropped and I had my passport back and he was scared I'd got the judge to turn the tables on him and have him locked up. I looked across at him and his girlfriend and I smiled at them. Then I picked up the local newspaper from the floor and pretended to read it.

We came in to land at the international airport, which was a first for me; normally you landed at the local airport and were driven around. As soon as the plane door opened, the accountant and his girlfriend grabbed their bags and made a run for it. I was right behind them and he looked back at me across the tarmac, sweat running pouring down his face. All he could see was me and five men that looked like lawyers. I think he thought they were with me and were going to arrest him! So he and his girlfriend started running for the terminal building and out of sight. This was the best I had felt for weeks.

A Case of Blood, Sweat and Tears

The last few days of my current five-week tour in Nigeria had gone very slowly. So, as soon as my back-to-back arrived, I headed straight to Port Harcourt domestic airport. As I stepped onto the aircraft steps, I felt all the previous week's problems lift from my shoulders. We landed at Lagos domestic airport – I still had the zoo to put up with, but this was not my first rodeo. My driver was there to meet me and he dropped me off at the Sheraton Hotel to kill a few hours before he would drive me over to the international airport for my flight home. This tour had been a nightmare from start to finish, what with client and employee problems to solve, and union negotiations that I always seemed to have to deal with rather than my French counterpart; he would put off meetings with to discuss salary and benefit packages for our Nigerian workforce until I was in the country. Anyway, enough of that.

I sat at the bar, drinking a strong gin and tonic. It was a great feeling knowing I had five weeks off to recharge my batteries. However, after having a meal and a few drinks, I got a little bit paranoid about missing my flight, so I decided to open my briefcase and double-check I had my passport and flight ticket. I had been dragging this case around the world for years; it was an aluminium Zero Halliburton I'd bought for $350 in Saudi Arabia. I loved that case... until the bloody thing wouldn't open. I tried the combination several times, but it still wouldn't open. Not a great feeling when I only had half an hour until my driver would be back to collect me for my flight! I could feel the panic set in. This was something I wasn't prepared for. I looked at the fire axe hanging on the wall next to the fire extinguishers. $350 or not... this was one option. I took a look at the back of the case and could see there was a steel rod running through the hinge – but how the hell was I going to remove it? The axe was still a contender.

I walked over to reception and asked if I could borrow a screwdriver. The maintenance man brought me a small one and I managed to push the rod halfway out, but it wouldn't come out any further. What to do? I took the case into the toilets, wedged the protruding rod in the jamb of the toilet door and pulled out it. At that moment, a guy walked in and I could read his mind: he thought I had stolen the case. Then my finger slipped over the sharp edge of the hinge. Blood everywhere. Now, bathed in sweat, I started trying to push my hand through the small gap at the back of the case. No luck – all I did was smear blood everywhere. There was a thick inner lining stopping me from getting hold of my passport and ticket.

So, back to reception, where I asked the receptionist if I could borrow a knife or a pair of scissors. She reached down into the drawer and handed me some scissors, as the blood began dripping onto the reception desk from under the toilet paper wrapped around my finger. "I'll get you a Band Aid," she said.

I cut through the thick material, pushed my hand through the case and caught hold of my passport and the ticket. I felt like bursting into tears. Then, from the corner of my eye, I saw my driver waving at me. With my passport and ticket in one hand and my briefcase tucked upside down under my other arm to stop everything inside falling out, I made my escape home.

I eventually managed to open the front of the case. The problem was the little slider you use to set your new code number had been somehow pushed to one side; when I closed the case, I spun the combination and the slider snapped back in place, with whatever random numbers were showing as my new code. The combination never worked again.

If you can't lock something, it's no good using it in Nigeria, so the case was put into retirement, although I have kept it all these years.

These are just a few of my stories from my time in Nigeria. There was never a dull moment.

During the second year of my contract with Frank's Nigeria, I closed down AVN, my video production company, and moved to Spain, where I bought an apartment in Calahonda on the Costa del Sol. For the remaining three years I carried on rotating back and forth on a five-week rotational schedule and during this period I met my third wife, Mariann, who, 25 years later, is still putting up with me. We met one wet Sunday afternoon in 1996 in a club called Fools Rush In. She was sitting with two friends of mine and they introduced me to her. I thought she was English – her accent sounded like she had gone to a private school – but no, Mariann was Danish and grew up and went to school in Sweden. She was a Scandinavian beauty! This was the first time in a long time a woman had interested me, other than just wanting sex with someone. We got on like a house on fire and one year later, we moved in with each other.

Mariann would get upset every time I returned to Nigeria and, after all the problems and the uncertainty about how long I would be stuck there, she asked if I could get a country manager's job somewhere else, so we could be together. I talked to Keith Vuillemont, my boss, and told him I was interested in moving to a new location with Mariann. Keith said he would look into it.

He called me back a couple of days later asking if I would be interested in the Brunei country manager job, adding that it was a married status contract. Mariann was excited about the move, even though it meant she would have to give up her art business. And there was another problem. After two failed marriages, I wasn't in a rush to get married for a third time – and Mariann wasn't in any hurry either. However, to be able to live together in Brunei we would have to get married for visa reasons. So, we were married at the British Council in Gibraltar, in the same room as John Lennon and Yoko Ono, with two very good friends, Sue and John Leech, as witnesses. I felt uncomfortable that this was Mariann's first marriage and she wasn't having a big white wedding in a nice church, but time was short. So we bit the bullet, and, with marriage certificate in hand, we were ready for our new life together in Asia.

Brunei Darussalam, 1999

Frank's had an exclusive five-year TRS contract with Brunei Shell Petroleum (BSP) and there was some ad hoc offshore work now and then with Elf Aquitaine. I had worked with both companies before and out of the two of them, I knew Shell would be very demanding. I had worked as a technician on the North Sea Shell Brent field and I knew they could be difficult to work for; their standards were high and they pushed for excellence in drilling technology and safety.

I arrived in Brunei on a three-month visit visa and was told this would be changed during the three months to a work visa. Mariann was scheduled to arrive once my work visa was completed. In the meantime, she would organise renting out our apparent in Spain.

Brunei is located on the northern coast of the island of Borneo and the country is completely surrounded by eastern Malaysia. Apart from the coastline, most of the country's biotopes constitute tropical rain forest, with an annual average temperature of 26-28°C and an annual rainfall of 2,500-5,000mm. Brunei is ruled by the Sultan of Brunei who, at this time, was the richest man in the world. The country is Muslim and, as with Saudi Arabia, is a dry country, i.e., no alcohol, pubs and nightclubs. In Brunei, there is no income tax, because most of the state's money comes from oil taxes. There is also a large welfare system offering free medical care, food and housing subsidies.

I arrived in Brunei and was picked up by the outgoing country manager, Drew Gardenier, an American who had been promoted to operations manager for the Far East and would be based in the regional office in Singapore. The drive from Bandar Seri Begawan, the capital city, took about an hour and a half. On arriving at the Frank's office in Kuala Belait, I was introduced to my secretary, Zaiton, and then to the directors of PTAS, Edmond and Haji, our Bruneian agents whose office and warehouse complex Frank's operated from. Drew told me I had an interview with Henk Westerink, the Shell Brunei drilling manager. The year before, Frank's had been awarded a five-year contract and there was a clause in it that said that, should there be a change of country manager, the new incumbent would have to be vetted and accepted by BSP (Brunei Shell Petroleum) before taking up their new position. My interview with Henk went well. He too had worked in Nigeria and the North Sea in the past, and he told me he was retiring and a new drilling manager would be taking over the job during the next month or two.

The next day, Drew left for Singapore to look around for a berth for his boat, so I was thrust into my new job with very little handover. I asked Drew if he had left me any handover notes. "No," he replied. "This is not your first rodeo. Any problems you can't handle, give me a call." I was lucky that I had inherited an excellent service supervisor: Hiram Blackledge was an American in his forties, a giant of a man but very quietly spoken. He had vast oilfield knowledge and had worked worldwide for Frank's in a number of locations over the years.

The next day, I had my first Shell morning drilling meeting. These meetings ran from 7 am every day of the year and you would move from one superintendent's office to the next, meeting all the country managers for the drilling and service companies to discuss drilling programmes and any downtime encountered in the last 24 hours on both offshore and onshore land rigs. I was about to walk into my office when Zaiton told me there was a British guy called Steve waiting for me. Steve told me that John Wheeler, the Far East regional manager, had sent him from Singapore "just in case I wasn't a good fit for Shell," in which case he was ready to step in. What the fuck!

I phoned John Wheeler in Singapore. "I'm settling in OK, thanks," I told him. "I aced the interview with BSP and I don't need anyone muddying the waters in Brunei. I don't think Shell or our local partners need to know that Frank's has so little faith in my ability to take up the position as county manager!"

"That's great, Les!" John said. "I am glad your interview went well. Put Steve on the phone."

Steve left for Singapore the next day and within a week was working for Halliburton in the Middle East. I hadn't met or worked for Wheeler, so I gave him the benefit of the doubt. However, I followed up with a phone call to Drew. I was still pissed off about Wheeler's antics and told Drew I was ready to pack my bags if there was any more shit. Drew told me to hang fire: there were a lot of changes going to happen soon and one of them was that John Wheeler was transferring to Dubai as VP for the Far and Middle East, while my old boss, Dick

Rader, would become the new Far East regional manager. This was excellent news. Dick and I had worked well together in Dubai during the 80s – but Dick was only to stay in Singapore for a month before flying back to Houston, never to return, thanks to an argument between himself and John Wheeler.

John Walker, who Drew replaced as the Far East operations manager, was sent back from Dubai as the regional manager. John and I had some history, dating back to when he was a CAM technician working for me in Aberdeen. He was a very determined guy, focused on climbing the corporate ladder, whatever it took – and I don't think he ever appreciated my way of working.

During the first week, I was asked by one of the Shell superintendents what I thought of Brunei. "I like it," I said. "I haven't seen one dead body since I got here!"

Brunei was one of the best overseas assignments for Shell employees, especially if they had young children. Shell had its own international school, which was also available to expat service company children; its own hospital and dental surgery; a golf course, sailing club and swimming pool; a supermarket – at that time, Shell staff were allowed to buy alcohol and pork there; and a very nice clubhouse and restaurant on the Belait River. Shell employees lived on their own kampong complex in Seria, which was close to the main BSP offices. Not a bad life. The only thing with Brunei was that every day was like Groundhog Day – or, as Hiram would say, "There's time and there's Brunei time." What I didn't realise until I arrived was that Shell had meetings to organise meetings; well, it seemed that way.

The Shell drilling department was known as a trial ground for the latest drilling equipment in their quest to drill deeper and cheaper. Shell pioneered long reach wells in the Champion West field and, later, drilled the first snake well in Brunei on the Iron Duke field, the deepest SMART completion in the world. Shell was a pioneer in using collective service companies' knowledge. In Brunei, the drilling and service company staff formed the Menang Team, who would meet each Friday morning and, in turn, you would present your company's latest technology to the group. Shell also carried out DWOPs (Drilling Well On Paper) and CWOPs (Completing Well On Paper) for each well to be drilled and followed up with an After Action Review meeting.

I was also on the Drilling Steering Committee, held once a month and consisting of the BSP drilling manager, his superintendents and all the service company country managers. Now, I might not have taken the job if I'd known what was expected of me. It wasn't the meetings that frightened me – I can stand up like the best of them and tell groups of people about Frank's equipment. NO, IT WAS THE FUCKING FLIP CHART! During the four and a half years I worked in Brunei, I somehow managed not to have to stand up and write the highlights and lowlights, tasks and targets on the flip chart for all in the room to see. I knew if I was put in this situation I would freeze in front of my colleagues and look like a fool – just like when my school teacher made me stand up and read a passage from a book in front of the class. I made sure I was never the first or the last to enter a meeting, just in case they asked me to take notes on the board. I used video and PowerPoint if it was my turn to present topics like safety or new company equipment; I was good with a video camera and video editing and graphics software, and I would spend a lot of time rehearsing the presentations.

During one steering group meeting, it was decided to hold a team building exercise: climbing Mount Kinabalu, the tallest mountain in Malaysia. The mountain is located in the state of Sabah, East Malaysia, on the island of Borneo. Part of the group signed up to climb to the top and stay overnight to watch the sun rise the next morning; I was in the group that climbed halfway up and back down in time for a good meal and further bonding at the bar.

At the end of the weekend, the group met up in one of the hotel's board rooms and the first thing I saw was a fucking flip chart. Each of the team members was given a sheet of paper with the list of topics to be discussed. My name was down as the facilitator, taking notes of the meeting during the afternoon session. After lunch, I told one of the Shell superintendents that I had a migraine and needed to lie down in a dark room, so I wouldn't be at the afternoon session. This was not my finest hour. The thing is, if I wasn't dyslexic, I would have been the first to put my hand up to be the facilitator; I mean, I like being the centre of attention.

There were always lots of parties and Mariann and I were invited to all the BSP and other service company events. Frank's was known for BBQs and we would have up to 40 people attend – and most would stay to the bitter end. Hiram was a BBQ king: steaks, catfish, chips, corn; you name it, he could cook it and he put so much effort into the meal. And of course we always had plenty of slabs of beer and boxes of wine to wash it all down with. I would make a call to our black-market associates for the beer; they would make a drop within an hour of ordering. But the wine was another story. I used to drive over the border to East Malaysia, to the second largest city of Miri. The road from Kuala Belait was flat and narrow, with one bridge and a ferry crossing. We would buy the wine at a duty-free store located just past the border post, or sometimes we would spend a weekend at a four-star hotel, where we would sit around the pool, drinking and eating good seafood. Life was good.

Kuala Belait was a sleepy town but it did have a couple of good restaurants. We usually entertained clients in one of three places that allowed us to take our own ice box full of beer and keep it out of sight under the table. The Orchid Room was a Thai Restaurant, where we would fill up a large teapot with beer and drink it out of cups; the Buccaneer was a steak house and you would always see several cheese platters itemized on the food bill, which was what they called Irish coffees; and finally, Mariann and I fondly remember the best Chinese food we have ever tasted at Jolene's.

One Christmas Day, I drove to the Shell complex for the morning meeting, only to find the car park full of cars. Being Christmas Day, I thought this was funny. I entered the drilling office, which was packed with all the BSP drilling staff, service company managers and their supervisors. I learned that one of the Smedvig Rigs, the West Menang, had had to pull away from the platform with the derrick still in place over the well; this was because of an uncontrolled well problem. No one was injured but it would take a second rig to bring the well under control by drilling a relief well to divert pressure. Shell hired an engineering company from Texas that specialized in directorial relief wells; they would bring the well under control, resulting in no need for a costly clean-up to the environment and Shell Brunei keeping its positive corporate image.

Towards the end of my second two-year contract, I was able to renew the TRS contract with BSP for a further five years. Mariann and I had made a lot of good friends during our time in Brunei. Mariann had put on a few exhibitions of her art, both in Brunei and East Malaysia, and sold a lot of her work to Shell and service company expats; I am sure to this day there are families moving around the world, adorning the walls of their homes with her artwork. And I had renewed my love of video production now that digital video equipment and software were at an affordable cost to be used as a hobby.

Unlike in Nigeria, there weren't any visits from the government authorities, police, immigration, army or the like; no corruption or riots to put you at risk. The only close encounter I had with danger was at the start of one Muslim holiday, Eid Al-Ahda, celebrated at the end of the month of Ramadan. Sunny, one of my Bruneian technicians, came into my office and told me he would not go offshore during the holiday. He had been booked to go offshore the next day and we were already short of technicians, because four of them had filled out vacation request forms. As I told Sunny he would have to go on the job, I could see the pupils of his eyes getting bigger and bigger. I had heard rumours that Sunny was taking Shabu (crystal meth). He started to get very upset and screamed at me that he would not go on the job.

All of a sudden, he jumped on top of my desk and leaped at me. I jumped up and got a hold of his head and put him in a full nelson. Sunny was a short guy but he was powerful and very muscular – and twenty years younger than me. He was wiggling and kicking; I managed to get him out into Zaiton's room, where he knocked over her desk, papers flying everywhere, telephone on the floor. This went on for a few minutes. Some of the other technicians ran into the office to see what all the commotion was about. I let go of the headlock, pushed Sunny towards the office door and told him to go home and that he was sacked.

He left the room. A minute later he was back, shaking a machete at me and screaming that he was going to kill me. The technicians in the room were all shouting at him to go home and one of them, a tall Malaysian called Ravin, put himself between us and told him to go. The next thing I knew, Sunny turned on his heels and ran out of the office.

I looked around the room. "Your nose is bleeding," Zaiton said. I looked down at my shirt. All the buttons had been ripped off, one of the sleeves was hanging off and it was covered in blood.

Once I had calmed down, I decided to go down to the police station and report the incident. But when I walked into the station, I could see Sunny had beaten me there; he was sitting there with his wife. I talked to the policeman on the desk, who asked me to come through to meet his sergeant. I made a brief statement and he said he would visit me at my office later that afternoon. To cut a long story short, Sunny was dismissed; he had previously been in trouble with the police, GBH (grievous bodily harm). Our agents wanted to press charges against him, but in the end, I decided not to. He had lost his job and, Kuala Belait being such a small place, he would have a problem getting employment with anyone else in the oilfield. Some years later, I was told that Sunny had killed himself by hitting a tree between Kuala Belait and Siri.

In 2003, I was promoted to Operations Manager Far East, taking Drew's job, and Drew was promoted to regional manager for the Far East, taking John Walker's job. Walker moved to Houston as a vice president and my job was taken by Billy Cooper, a technician who had worked for me in Aberdeen in the 90s. I always remember Billy reading the handover notes I had given him and saying, "Walker said you couldn't spell!"

Within two years, our long-term agent PTAS dumped Frank's for Weatherford, who moved all their oilfield services to Brunei and made PTAS their sole partner. Frank's moved to Amrtur Corporation – Amrtur was a well-established BSP provider – and stayed with them for a few years, before deciding to become a standalone Brunei Ltd company.

Frank's Singapore, 2003

We were to live in Singapore for the next 11 years and it was the best job I ever had. Mariann made many good friends over the years and set up her own art studio. She sold a lot of her etchings and lino prints through the largest art gallery in Singapore, Red Sea Gallery, and had a teaching job in the famous Singapore Taylor Print Institute, a dynamic creative workshop and contemporary art gallery committed to promoting artistic experimentation in the mediums of print and paper, which has become one of the most cutting-edge destinations for contemporary art in Asia. A happy wife is a happy life and I look back on this period in my life with fond affection. I was at home. We were always entertaining family and friends who visited Singapore. Lots to see and do. Visiting China Town and Little India; I think you could eat out every day of the year in a different restaurant.

I was on the road around 20 days a month. I had to visit our bases and clients in 14 countries in Asia, and this of course was determined by several factors: sales visits, problem solving and setting up new locations. Some of these countries had a full-time country manager and the rest were locations we would send personnel and equipment to from Singapore for the duration of the contract. The latter took up most of my time, with monthly safety meetings and problem solving, personnel and equipment issues and invoice enquiries.

We had a great staff in Singapore and Drew was a good guy to work for; he and I would travel a lot together.

After a couple of years, Hiram transferred from Brunei to Singapore as service supervisor and we also employed Winston Longue, a very smart young Singaporean, to take responsibility for all the quality assurances and safety issues that now made up a huge part of contract tenders. My four and a half years in Brunei had been a great training ground, for now all the oil companies had taken a leaf out of Shell's book and were running DWOPs and CWOPs for their upcoming wells. I had been taught by the best and would use this experience to add equipment to the contract that would save them time – and time is money, especially for deep-water rigs with a speed sheet of around a million dollars a day. The best thing, though, was that these oil companies always used their own facilitators, so there was no need for me to worry about the dreaded flip chart ever again.

Over the years, we would move house four times, a result of Singapore housing costs going up and coming down. I had a fixed contract allowance for house rental, which, when it came to renew our housing contract, meant if the house had gone up in price we would have to move to something cheaper, and if the housing costs had gone down, we could move to a better location. Drew never had this problem as he lived on a large boat in one of Singapore's marinas; not a bad lifestyle.

I was never in danger during these 11 years, except for the time I was visiting Jakarta. I was in our office, which was on three floors, having a meeting with Jim

Delaney, Frank's country manager, when the pictures on the walls started to shake. Then the building started shaking! Jim jumped to his feet. "Follow me outside," he said. "We are having an earthquake."

Halfway down the stairs, there was a huge vibration and the office swerved violently, then stopped. The quake was felt throughout Jakarta, although damage to the city was minimal. The quake had a magnitude of 7.0 Mw and was Indonesia's deadliest earthquake since the 2006 Pangandaran earthquake and tsunami; it would become known as the 2009 West Java earthquake.

Over the years, I embarrassed myself a couple of times. Once, while visiting Sakhalin in Russia, I was drinking with several of the BP drilling staff and someone spiked my drink. I felt dizzy and had to leave the bar; I peed myself before I could open the door to my room and slept until morning on top of the bed in my clothes. After that, I made sure I didn't take my eye off my drink. I said nothing the next day; I wasn't going to tell anyone what happened.

Another time, I was driving home from work and, just before the turning into my road, I noticed that a new shop had opened. There were fantastic arrangements of flowers and people inside drinking champagne. So I stopped outside and decided to buy Mariann a bunch of flowers from this new florist. I stood in the doorway and a Chinese lady asked me if I would like a drink. "No thanks," I said. "I just noticed you're open and I wanted to buy some of your flowers for my wife."

The lady smiled and said: "These flowers are from well-wishers on the opening of my new clinic." She handed me her business card. "Doctor Lee Lim – gynaecologist."

I took the card and said: "I will have my wife contact you."

Sometimes I would take Mariann with me on trips to places like China, Myanmar (Burma), Hong Kong and Australia. We have good memories of these places and the people we met.

During my years in Singapore I had several medical problems, but I must say that Singapore has some of the best hospitals in the world and I was lucky the company had good medical insurance.

But all good things must come to an end. The Mosing family had decided to take the company public and things were about to change. Drew had been taken very ill and was hospitalized for some weeks before they knew what was wrong with him; he had to spend some time away from his job. Now, over the years I had seen friends take sick leave or vacation, only to return to work to find out they had been laid off or transferred to a new location. In Drew's case, he was told he was being transferred to Brazil as Frank's Business and Development Manager. I asked Drew if I had a chance of the regional manager's position and he said no, Keith Mosing had said I was not being considered.

Drew was replaced by Doug Reid. Doug had worked for several PLCs and was well known by John Walker... I could see this was where the company was heading. Doug arrived and I had a discussion with him about my position with the company – and he left me in no doubt that my days as the operations manager for the Far East were coming to an end. I think things would have happened a lot faster than they did if Doug hadn't had to go into hospital for cancer surgery. I had been standing in for Drew for eight years whenever he was on vacation or while he was travelling, without any problems, and I ran the region until Doug returned to work with a clean bill of health a month later. However, shortly after Doug's return, my job was taken over by someone Frank's had headhunted from one of our PLC TRS competitors. I was told I could stay on in a new position, maybe in a training role.

Mariann and I had already decided that maybe it was time for me to take early retirement. She had returned home to Spain six months before my contract was due to finish, to set up her new art business on the Costa del Sol and take over the running of our three rental properties, which were currently managed by a third party. I talked over this new training role with her. It seemed obvious that Frank's wanted me out of Singapore, but we agreed that I really needed another two-year contract to add to our retirement nest egg. So I made enquiries with management and was offered the job of country manager in Saudi Arabia. I did my due diligence, phoning friends and asking what was going on with Frank's Saudi – and it wasn't good. I remembered when Frank's first began operating in Saudi, just after I moved from Dubai to Aberdeen, back in 1987. They opened the base with expat technicians and new equipment: power units, power tongs of all sizes, a couple of pick-up and lay-down units and a few diesel hammers, plus a fleet of personnel vehicles. But for some years now, the operation had been run from the Dubai regional office with only a Syrian service supervisor handling the day to day running. No money had been spent on the base or office and only infrequent visits were made by the Dubai management. However, they were still making a small profit.

Having lived previously in Saudi, I knew I would only take the job if I was allowed to live in Bahrain and commute over the causeway five days a week. There wasn't a queue waiting for the job, so I decided to play hardball. I managed to get a decent two-year contract from Ricky McFarlane, the Middle East regional manager, who once worked for me as a technician in Nigeria; he had come a long way in a short time. I managed to stay on a married contract on the same salary as Singapore, with two weeks off every six months and paid flights to and from Spain. I did a lot of research into where I wanted to live in Bahrain and I negotiated a very good housing allowance.

During the weeks leading up to my departure from Singapore, I had my birth and marriage certificates and any management training diplomas certified and rubber-stamped at a notary, before submitting them and the necessary forms to the Saudi Embassy for a business visa; once I was in the country, this would be changed to a residence/work visa.

Saudi Arabia Revisited, 2012

So, my overseas oilfield career had gone full circle and I would end it as I started, in Saudi Arabia. The packers had packed up my furniture and while it was on water to Bahrain, I travelled back to Spain to spend a month with Mariann, before heading off to Saudi to start my new two-year contract as country manager. After a good rest, I was ready to fly into Dhahran International airport, where, on arrival, I was picked up by the office driver, Peter. For many years he had been a technician but, now in his sixties, he was working his last couple of years before retirement as a driver.

We drove to the office in Al-Khobar. At first sight, I could see the place had changed completely. Dhahran and Al-Khobar seemed to have merged into one another, with new highways and overpasses and high-rise apartment blocks everywhere. There were still streets with the same old housing I used to live in, but Al-Khobar was now so much bigger. We arrived outside the Frank's complex to be greeted by two big green steel gates, but Frank's sign was nowhere to be seen. Peter sounded the car horn and a technician opened the gates and we drove in. At first sight, the yard looked a mess and as I walked into the office, I couldn't believe what I saw: a right fucking mess! I had been spoiled in the Far East – both the Brunei and Singapore offices were new and had all the latest in workshop and office equipment. Nothing had been spent on this complex since the eighties and the office was disgustingly dirty.

The other thing that hit me – and I should have been prepared for this – was that no females worked in the office. The Far East offices were full of very intelligent and good-looking women, but now I would see only male staff, accountants and secretaries. I was met by Ahsan, a slim Pakistani in his forties; he was the office administrator and would turn out to be very helpful during my stay in Saudi. He showed me the way to an office located right at the back of the building. There sat Khalid, the base service supervisor. Khalid was a Syrian, a short stubby guy also in his forties, and he had been in charge of the day to day running of the base for some years. I knew straight away he was going to be a handful and wouldn't like the idea of someone coming in and taking charge of the operation. I looked around his office. It was the largest in the building. He had a big office desk and there were two Hough sofas; one of them was a shocking pink and both had seen better days.

Khalid got up from his desk and, with a big smile on his face, put out his hand and welcomed me to Saudi Arabia. I thanked him and pointed out that this was not my first time in the country and that I had spent over four years working for Weatherford in Al-Khobar during the 80s. I told Khalid that I would be making a lot of changes to the operation but for now, I needed to check in at the Holiday Inn and I would need Peter to pick me up in the morning at 8 am. I had to stay at the hotel for a couple of weeks until my work visa was completed. Then I could apply for the exit re-entry permit required to drive back and forth over the causeway to Bahrain.

The next day, I evicted Khalid from his office and moved him into a smaller room with a view over the yard. He wasn't very happy. I wanted to split the big office into two rooms: one for me and one for the accounts department. I ordered two big trash skips and the first thing into them was the pink settee; the room they used as a kitchen had three cookers and two fridges that were disgusting, to say the least, so they also had to go. The guys working in the workshop hung up their clothes on nails outside in the yard and there was nowhere to wash and change. Having a changing room was a priority, and new lockers and washing facilities were installed.

I met with Sheikh Abdulaziz Ali Alturki, group chairman of Rawabi Holdings, who had been Frank's partner from the onset in the 80s. I also met his oilfield general manager, Ahmed Al Qabdeeb, and their Frank's account holder, Haitham Harfouche, the contracts' JV support manager. Frank's management, on the whole, were very wary of letting JV partners in to their day to day business and looked at partners as a form of tax. I always worked well with our partners: they were taking a percentage of the invoices; Rawabi were keen to work with me and I was happy with that. Ahmed and Haitham opened all kind of doors in Saudi Aramco for me – and getting my foot in the door enabled me to add new products and services to the contract.

Russia has the largest oil reserves in the world by landmass, with over 106 billion barrels of proven oil reserves within the country's borders, but Saudi Arabia has the Ghawar oilfield, which is the largest oilfield in the world, at 280km long and 40km wide. It's located in Saudi's Al Hasa Province. Aramco is the second largest state oil company in the world, with 150 rigs, and we shared the TRS work with two other international companies, Weatherford and Zamil Premier Casing Services.

My passport was stamped with my Saudi residency visa and an exit re-entry permit; it was time to make arrangements to move into my new home in Bahrain. Proceeding through the Saudi causeway passport and customs control point wasn't a problem and, at midday, it only took 15 minutes to pass through. Driving back over the causeway and checking in at the Bahrain passport customs border post took 30 minutes, so a total of 45 minutes in all, and then the 10-minute drive into Manama city centre. I booked myself into the Sheraton Hotel. Later that afternoon, I had a meeting with a visa agent who would help me sort out all the necessary paperwork to be able to live in Bahrain.

The next day, I was met at the hotel by an estate agent who drove me out to look at a few houses at Riffa Views, which was part of the Royal Golf Club complex. I settled for a new 4-bedroom house on Lagoon Avenue, overlooking the 9-hole and a short walk from the clubhouse. The Bahrain paperwork was all completed and a two-year lease signed on the house. The last thing I needed was a cheque from Dubai for my new company vehicle, a Ford Edge – a large 4x4 SUV, to give me some protection from the local nutcases on the road. In all the years I had worked overseas, this was the best housing and company car I'd ever had – and it felt good.

My daily routine was to wake up at 4.30 am and shower. Toast and coffee, then drive over the causeway, through both passport and customs border posts and arrive in my office before 6 am. I would leave Al-Khobar by 2.15 pm and be back home by 3.30 pm. And I did this five days a week. The reason for the early start was that if you went an hour later in the morning, it could take twice the time to cross over, and the same in the afternoon. So I stuck to these times unless I had late meetings with clients – and then I could be hours in a queue to get home.

Weekend and holiday crossings were not contemplated unless absolutely required, as the families living in Al-Khobar all wanted to spend time in Bahrain's children's water park or at the cinema, maybe having a glass of wine or beer with a meal – all not available in Saudi.

Saudi Aramco

Before I received my residence visa, every time I went to Aramco I had to register at the security visitor centre when I needed to visit anyone in Dhahran. But now, with all my paperwork in order, I could apply for an Aramco ID pass that would let me into Dhahran, Abqaiq, Ras Tannura and Manifa drilling offices. I filled out all the necessary forms and the next morning I drove over to the Dhahran security office and handed in my application. They took my photo and fingerprints and the security officer said, "You've had an ID pass from Aramco before."

"Yes," I said, "but that was 30 years ago."

"Take a look at my computer screen," he said, and there were my fingerprints on the screen, along with an old ID number from 1981! I was issued with a new ID pass with my old ID number on it; obviously nothing gets past Aramco.

During my two-year contract, I made it my mission to introduce new Frank's technology that would save Aramco money and make Frank's a lot of money. Khalid would look after the equipment load outs and our 40 technicians: 25 Syrians and 15 Saudis from the eastern region of Qatif; these technicians were Shia, who make up only 15% of the main population, the rest being Sunni Muslims. Over the years, Qatif has seen violent clashes between Shia demonstrators and security forces and the reason we employed guys from Qatif was they were not afraid of hard work. I determined to do my best to improve the monthly revenues going forward; that was my job.

A few years earlier, Frank's had purchased a company specialising in manufacturing down hole drilling tools, DSTR, HI and CBI tools. To introduce these tools to Aramco, I needed some down hole tool engineers to be available to attend meetings in Dhahran. These engineers would come from the UK and USA and, seeing that I had plenty of rooms in my house, they would fly to Bahrain and stay with me. During their stay they would accompany me each evening to the golf clubhouse for dinner and drinks, and cross over with me to Al-Khobar for meetings each morning before flying back home from Bahrain.

Aramco was very interested in these drilling tools but it would take many field trials before we got to the stage of signing a contract. Aramco was operating 150 drilling rigs off and onshore. Some of these rigs were operated on a turnkey contract with Schlumberger and Halliburton and I managed to sign contracts with both these companies, plus ENSCO Drilling for TRS services.

By the time I left Saudi, I would have doubled the original monthly revenue.

Bahrain

The year before I arrived in Bahrain, the country had been subjected to Bloody Thursday, four days of uprising as part of the Arab Spring. Bahrain Shia were the larger of the population, numbering around 60%, but the country was ruled by the Sunni minority Royal Family. Bahrain security forces launched a pre-dawn raid to clear the Pearl Roundabout in Manama of the Shia protesters camped there, most of whom were asleep in tents at the time. Four were killed and about three hundred injured. The event led some to demand even more political reform than there had been before, including calls for an end to the reign of the Sunni King Hamad bin Isa Al Khalifa.

The main roads from my house to the causeway were heavily protected by security forces; at night, the whole place was lit up like a fairground, with their blue lights flashing from one side of the island to the other. Some days you could be held up in long queues because of roadblock inspections. I once got lost in one of the Shia towns located close to the now demolished Pearl Roundabout. There were lots of people in the streets and it seemed like every house had a black flag flying outside it, but no one gave me any problems, there were no security forces in sight and I managed to get home unscathed.

I just loved my new house. My container had arrived and all it needed was someone to make it look like home.

Mariann arrived for a two-week visit, three months into my contract, and she helped me sort the house out and make it homely.

To pass the time, I played on the 9-hole golf course. The 9th hole was right in front of my house but, having said that and after several lessons from the golf pro, over the years my handicap never improved.

Dubai

Ricky made a trip to Saudi every couple of months and was happy with the way the base had improved, but I had to fight tooth and nail to get funding for all the projects required to bring this unit up to standard. Dubai was spending huge amounts of money on a new office/workshop complex in the Jebel Ali industrial area and was installing a land rig and drilling a hole to be able to run training courses for the regional TRS technicians. Guy Hustinx was from Belgium; he was in his sixties and, like me, had been with the company for over 30 years. He had also started off as a technician and had just moved to Dubai as Middle East and West Africa Vice President.

Guy called a regional managers' meeting in Dubai, which suited me as I always enjoyed trips there; it was a break from the daily drive over to Saudi and a chance to meet up with old friends. Guy had organised a few managers' nights out: one was a visit to see Cirque du Soleil at the Trade Centre Exhibition Arena; another was a BBQ at his home.

On my way back from the meeting, I was sitting in the airport lounge when I looked across at people waiting to board the Bahrain flight and saw a guy I was certain was Dave Piper, an old friend of mine. I walked over to the man and said: "Hi, Dave!"

"Sorry, do I know you?" he said. And then the penny dropped and I realised that it wasn't him, as Dave would now be twenty years older. I apologised and boarded the plane. I had just joined Facebook so, when I got back to the house, I opened it up and put Dave's name in the search box. Bloody hell, he came up – and he was living in Bahrain. Spooky! Dave was running his own company, linking oil service companies around Europe that wanted to do business in the Middle East with local joint venture partners and presenting them to oil companies such as Bahrain's Babco, who had nodding donkey production wells all around my house and the golf course.

Dave and I would meet up most weekends for dinner and drinks, either in Riffa Views or Manama, where he lived. If I was going to Manama, I would take a taxi to the city so I could have a good drink. One night, we had finished dinner at a fancy restaurant and landed up doing a pub and club crawl. I eventually took a taxi home in the early hours – only to find that I had lost all my keys: house, office and car! Luckily, I had put a spare house key under the front doormat so I was able to get inside, but my spare car key was in the office in Saudi. And that would be a right mess to sort out, as someone would have to drive over the causeway to bring the key back to me and this could take days if no one had a current exit re-entry visa.

I phoned Dave right away and told him the story. "No problem, Les. I'll go out and find them," he said. I was thinking he would sleep first, but not Dave. Several hours later, my phone rang. It was Dave. "I got your keys. They were tucked into the side of a seat in one of the clubs we visited."

Now that's what you call a mate. "Lunch is on me at the clubhouse!" I said. The Royal Golf Course on a Saturday ran a big buffet, where there would be more than a hundred people eating great food washed down with champagne and enjoying good live entertainment.

To this day, Dave and I still have a laugh about our Bahrain night outs during our weekly Facetime chats.

Houston

Over my forty years in the oilfield, I was lucky enough to have had the chance to visit Texas and

Lafayette, where I met and worked with some great people. My first trip was in 1983 with Weatherford. Hartmut decided I needed some product training in Houston and I stayed there for three weeks. During my visit, the annual Offshore Technology Conference (OTC) was taking place. This was a huge event and I would attend many more over the years.

I always remember my first time in Houston. As I left the terminal building, I said to myself, *Yes, everything IS bigger in America!* The cars, the highways, even the businesses seemed to be on a much bigger scale. Car dealers had hundreds of new cars on their lots, mounted on top of high poles, standing on rooftops and hanging from walls. It was a little overwhelming.

Visiting restaurants was so different. The waiters worked on tips and the Americans can tip – unlike like the British. Fifteen per cent was added to the final bill without a second thought. Mind you, the waiters worked hard; they knew who ordered what and never got it wrong, and the meals were good and plenty of it.

I remember at the oil show, Weatherford had minibuses circulating the grounds with the company logo on the side. I waved at one and the driver stopped. As I opened the door, I could hear an argument between the four guys on the bus. I jumped in and slid the door closed. The bus moved on and I looked up to see the four guys were the president and three vice presidents of Weatherford. "Hi!" I said. "I am Les Ellis of Weatherford Saudi Arabia." They all looked at me in silence. We arrived at the next stop and I got the fuck out of there. I thought I might be in trouble after hearing them arguing but then again, they were all talking German and my name probably went in one ear and out of the other – but you never know.

That was my only Houston trip for Weatherford. Frank's always put on a lot of events during OTC, and I was lucky to visit many times and always felt welcome. Frank's held a crawfish boil on the second night of OTC, with over 3,000 people attending, over 10,000 pounds of crawfish, 3,000 servings of jambalaya and lots of beer and Cajun music. It made for a good night out.

After my mother died and I had returned from my sabbatical working for myself at AVN, I was in Houston for OTC when all the Frank's managers were flown in on three of the Frank's jets from Sugar Land airport to Weatherford Texas for the opening of Frank's new centralizer plant. This was the second time I had been to this manufacturing plant; the first time it was owned by Weatherford Lamb. I got off the plane and walked into the terminal building with the other Managers. I could see Keith and Donald Mosing, who had just arrived on a different plane. Donald looked straight at me. Then he walked over to me, put his arms around me and said: "Welcome back, Les. I am very sorry to hear about your mother." Now, you would never have a PLC president do this; this is the difference between a PLC and a family company and the reason why Frank's held onto their employees, some for over forty years.

Not all my trips to Houston were for work. Before I purchased my apartment in Spain, I was looking in other places, including France and Texas. I had been invited to stay with my old boss Dick Rader and his wife Sharon during one of my times off from Nigeria, and Dick had a few trips lined up. The first was to NASA's Johnson Space Center, where we were able to visit the inside of the space shuttle; it was a fantastic day out. Dick also had to make a visit to Dallas to visit Exxon Mobil. Now, I said before that Mr Frank had always said, "Look after the engineers and you will always be welcome when they become superintendent or drilling manager," and never a truer word was said. Here we were, walking the corridors of power in the headquarters of one of the biggest oil companies in the world and visiting guys we knew from our Dubai days, guys who had played on the Frank's softball team and were really happy to see us.

Later that afternoon, Dick said: "How about visiting Southfork Ranch?" It was the setting for the television series *Dallas* and I sat on JR's bed. Apparently, the only scenes filmed at the ranch were in JR's bedroom and around the swimming pool; the rest were filmed in California.

I have fond memories of the visits to Houston and the nights out with Dick Rader, Maxi Gremillion and Keith Mosing. I would like to say many thanks to all my colleagues worldwide who played a big part in my development within the company.

Close to Death Again

One morning, I awoke as usual at 4.30 and by 5.30 am, I was about a mile from the Bahrain border post. At the time, the authorities were searching every truck that entered or exited Bahrain, looking for explosives and weapons. The backed-up trucks were taking up the hard shoulder and the first lane, leaving me only one lane to drive in. All the drivers were out of their cabs, standing or sitting along the roadside as they chatted to each other; some were even standing in the central reservation.

Suddenly, I could see a car approaching very fast, flashing his lights for me to get out of the way. But there was nowhere to go: there was a car 50 feet in front of me and lorries to the side of me. But he kept coming at me at some speed. He was now close to my bumper and I could see a gap in the trucks, so I moved over, just in time for him to pass me. I had to move over back into the outside lane as there were trucks in front of me and as I did, this dumb fucker hit the car in front of me right up the ass. The car was pushed into the trucks parked on the inside lane and the white Toyota that hit him went up in the air about 8 feet, somersaulted over and over and landed in the central reservation, hitting two truck drivers.

There were men running everywhere. I managed to slow down and pick my way through the broken parts of car lying all over the road. I pulled over to the side of the road and saw customs officers running to the scene. Now, I knew that, as an expat, you shouldn't get involved with Muslim dead and injured; I had always been told that if you were attending to an injured person, you stood a chance of being held responsible if they died.

After about five minutes, one of the officers came over to me. I told him it was the driver of the white Toyota that caused the accident and he said: "Don't get involved. Drive away."

The next day, in the Royal Golf Club coffee shop, I read a report in the daily Bahrain English newspaper concerning the accident. Two Pakistani truck drivers had been killed and two badly injured. And this wasn't the first or the last time I would see Saudis driving like maniacs after leaving Bahrain nightclubs, driving drunk and tired. The one thing I had learned from working in the Middle East over the years was that they all drove their cars like mad men and you always had to keep a good eye on your rear-view mirror.

My contract was coming to an end. The management in Dubai were aware of this and had asked me to sign a further two-year contract, but I made it clear that I wasn't interested. Frank's had changed a lot after it became a public company. Guys who had worked their way into executive positions and had been with the company for decades but didn't have a university education were let go and those coming up to retirement had left, having had enough. The company no longer had a family feel to it. Just before the PLC listing, long-term employees had been given a modest number of shares in the company. Management were given shares according to their positions – country managers, regional managers and vice presidents – but what upset me was that it didn't seem to matter how long you had worked for the company, you were still only given shares according to your job position.

At the last moment, Ricky found Harry Steiner to replace me. We managed a few weeks of induction and on the day my contract finished, I said my goodbyes to my clients and staff and crossed over the causeway for the last time, leaving the base in a much better state than I found it. The next week was spent packing up the house and having a last night out with Dave in Manama. And then I flew to Dubai for my end of contract negotiations with management.

That night, I was taken out for dinner with Ricky McFarlane, Guy Hustinx VP, Nick Jain VP, the head of regional finance, and BJ Latiolais, Executive VP Operations, based in Houston. It was a good send off. Now all I had to do was collect my Golden Handshake.

The next morning I met with Ricky and Guy. The conversation began with me discussing the Saudi base: how I had found it and what it was like today, what equipment and services I had added to the table and the fact I had doubled the revenue during my time here. The first negotiation was based on the end of my second-year contract; this was the same amount as the year before and we agreed on that. The next was for the end of service agreement. I had worked for Frank's in many locations and over the years I had brought a lot of value to the company and been a loyal employee. They asked me what I thought I should be given and the look of surprise on their faces told me it wasn't what they were thinking. I had an idea what others had been given, but they came back to me with a figure half what I wanted.

"No, just keep it," I said. Again, they looked at me in astonishment. Then they said they needed to go away and discuss this with the finance department, for some reason. But I had an ace in my hand: they had to get me to sign an NCA, a Non-Compete Agreement, which legally binds a current or former employee from competing with an employer for some period of time after employment ceases. They sat back down and offered me a further 25% and I signed the NCA. I'm not sure, but I think they were a little pissed off with me... We shook hands and that was that.

I took a taxi from the regional office to my hotel, packed my things and headed for the airport to catch a flight to Denmark. Mariann and I had decided we'd had enough of living in hot countries and, six months before the end of my contract, we started looking for a new home. We decided to purchase a house on a small island in the south of Denmark, in Møn, where Mariann's family lived.

Epilogue

So, I've written a book on my life in the oil industry. If you had told me, at the age of 15, that in my septuagenarian year I would publish a book, or even read one, I would have said you're mad! If I could travel back in time, I would love to drop off a copy of my book on the table of the teacher's panel and say to them, "I did travel the world and I did get paid a lot of money. So don't discourage but encourage those with learning disabilities to follow their dreams."

Appendix 1:
Drilling Crew Job Descriptions

Roustabout

The roustabout is typically the entry level position when starting offshore and can be compared with a deck hand on a ship. The roustabout is responsible for carrying out work in connection with loading/unloading operations, general maintenance and cleaning jobs, and assistance to the drill floor crew.

Roughneck

The roughneck is responsible for pipe handling, casing and drilling equipment on the drill floor as well as carrying out maintenance on the equipment. The roughneck also makes and breaks rotary connections using rig tongs, handles tubular goods, elevators and slips, and operates semi-automated pipe-handling machines. Additionally, the roughneck participates in the daily cleaning, housekeeping and maintenance work on the drill floor and in the shale shaker room.

Derrickman

The derrickman supervises and inspects the mud processing areas and ensures that these are kept clean and tidy, and that maintenance on the equipment is carried out in accordance with procedures. The derrickman pays special attention to the valves and pumps in the mud and cementing systems.

He is also responsible for working in the derrick and operates at heights of 90 ft from the rig floor. The derrickman racks back the drill collars, heavy weight and standard drill pipe into metal storage fingers when running and pulling pipe in and out of the rotary table (hole). His operational area is called the monkey board.

Mud Engineers (Mudloggers)

Mud engineers usually go out and check the shakers for rock samples that have circulated from the bottom. They separate the rock from the drilling fluid and take it into an onsite lab where they dry out the samples and label them according to depth. They then look at the samples and analyse what kind of rock they have at a certain depth. This helps determines what depth that type of rock was encountered. The mud Engineer is also assisted by the derrickman once the drill bit is making hole; he services the mud pumps and is in charge of chemical inventory.

Tong Operator

The tong operator has been trained on all company power tongs and power units, both diesel and electric models. He is responsible for making sure all the equipment used is in a safe condition, fit for purpose and that the torque gauge has been installed correctly.

He works with the stabber to make sure the pin and box connections are not crossed and that the right make-up torque is applied, as per the manufacturer's specifications.

Torque Turn Operator

The torque turn operator is responsible for discussing the casing running programme with the company man, making sure the correct information is put into the torque turn computer program and that his load cell and connection are rigged up correctly. He is also responsible for repairing the computer should there be a problem; normally there is full back-up equipment on the rig.

He monitors each connection make-up or break-out and enters any relevant comments. He is responsible for any bad connection being run downhole so, when in doubt, he will throw the joint out, back to the pipe deck.

Casing Stabbers

Casing stabbers are technicians who work 40 ft up from the rotary table on a movable platform called the stabbing board. Their job is to guide the 40 ft joint of casing into the box connection and make sure they are inline before the tong operation starts rotating the pipe, eliminating the chance of a crossed joint of pipe.

The stabber is there also to guide the elevator over the top of the casing and setting the elevator around the joint ready to lift the string and run it into the hole.

Assistant Driller

The assistant driller supervises the work done on the drill floor and all other work in connection with the drilling operations. The assistant driller position is regarded as a trainee position to achieve competency to work as a driller.

Driller

The driller is responsible for supervising and carrying out the drilling and well control and other work in connection with the drilling operations. He must ensure safe operation of the drilling control system, drawworks; pipe handling systems; mud circulating systems and blow-out prevention (BOP) equipment in accordance with the requirements specified in the operating procedures.

Tool Pusher

The tool pusher is the overall person responsible for drilling operations as outlined by the drilling section leader. He ensures that all drilling operations are carried out in accordance with the fixed programme and supervises the drill crew and drilling equipment as well as the deck crew and other ongoing work on board the rig. Basically, it's his way or the highway.

Casing Crew

The casing hand is responsible for:

Assisting with casing/tubing operations involving various types/sizes of tubulars and utilizing varying types/sizes of company's equipment.

Ensuring that all pre-job checks are conducted and that the full equipment package is ready for the job.

Interfacing, as required, with company reps, crew pusher, tool pusher, drill crew, drilling engineer and third parties to ensure that all well acceptance criteria for the installation have been met.

Working as a crew member during the actual

installation/work and has been trained and competent in equipment for the job, power units, power tongs, torque turn computer, stabbing board installation.

Ensuring and assisting with the safe rig up and operation of equipment in accordance with company's procedures and customer instructions.

Assisting and at times leading with employee development and training for onshore/offshore work with feedback to crew pusher on the progress and level of personnel competency.

Serving as onsite safety representative, who will follow and ensure that all other personnel onsite will conduct operations in accordance with company's and customer HSE procedures and policies.

Learning and becoming conversant with all company's philosophies, policies, and procedures including safety, quality, operational, and environmental training.

In other words: YOU GOTTA BE FUCKING GOOD.

Appendix 2:
Rig Floor Definitions

Derrick

A derrick is a lifting device composed at minimum of one guyed mast, as in a gin pole, which may be articulated over a load by adjusting its guys. Most derricks have at least two components, either a guyed mast or self-supporting tower, and a boom hinged at its base to provide articulation, as in a stiffleg derrick. The most basic type of derrick is controlled by three or four lines connected to the top of the mast (crown block), which allow it both to move laterally and cant up and down. To lift a load, a separate line runs up and over the mast with a hook on its free end, as with a crane.

Forms of derricks are commonly found aboard ships. Some large derricks are mounted on dedicated vessels and known as floating derricks and sheerlegs. The term derrick is also applied to the framework supporting a drilling apparatus in an oil rig exploration platform.

Rotary Table

A rotary table is a mechanical device on a drilling rig that provides clockwise (as viewed from above) rotational force to the drill string to facilitate the process of drilling a borehole. Rotary speed is the number of times the rotary table makes one full revolution in one minute (rpm).

The rotary table is also called a turntable. Most rotary

tables are chain driven. These chains resemble very large bicycle chains. The chains require constant oiling to prevent burning and seizing.

Virtually all rotary tables are equipped with a rotary lock. Engaging the lock can either prevent the rotary from turning in one particular direction, or from turning at all. This is commonly used by crews in lieu of using a second pair of tongs to make up or break out pipes.

The rotary bushings are located at the centre of the rotary table. These can generally be removed in two separate pieces to facilitate large items, e.g. drill bits, to pass through the rotary table.

The large gap in the centre of the rotary bushings is referred to as the 'bowl' due to its appearance. The bowl is where the slips are set to hold up the drill string during connections and pipe trips as well as the point the drill string passes through the floor into the wellbore. The rotary bushings connect to the kelly bushings to actually induce the spin required for drilling.

Drawworks

A drawworks is the primary hoisting machinery component of a rotary drilling rig. Its main function is to provide a means of raising and lowering the traveling block. The wire-rope drill line winds on the drawworks drum and over the crown block to the travelling block, allowing the drill string to be moved up and down as the drum turns. The segment of drill line from the drawworks to the crown block is called the 'fast line'. The drill line then enters the first sheave of the crown block and makes typically 6 to 12 passes between the crown block and travelling block pulleys for mechanical advantage. The line then exits the last sheave on the crown block and is fastened to a derrick leg on the other side of the rig floor. This section of drill line is called the 'dead line'.

A modern drawworks consists of five main parts: the drum, the power source, the reduction gear, the brake, and the auxiliary brake. The apparatus can be powered by AC or DC, or the drawworks may be connected directly to internal combustion engines using metal chain-like belts. The number of gears could be one, two or three speed combinations. The main brake, usually operated manually by a long handle, may be a friction band brake, a disc brake or a modified clutch. It serves as a parking brake when no motion is desired. The auxiliary brake is connected to the drum, and absorbs the energy released as heavy loads are lowered. This brake may use eddy current rotors or water-turbine-like apparatus to convert the kinetic energy of the moving load to heat and dissipate it. Power catheads (winches) located on each side provide the means of actuating the tongs used to couple and uncouple threaded pipe members. Outboard catheads can be used manually with ropes for various small hoisting jobs around the rig.

The drawworks often has a pulley drive arrangement on the front side to provide turning power to the rotary table, although on many rigs the rotary table is independently powered.

Drill Floor

The drill floor is the heart of any drilling rig. This is the area where the drill string begins its trip into the earth. It is traditionally where joints of pipe are assembled, as well as the BHA (bottom hole assembly), drilling bit, and various other tools. This is the primary work location for roughnecks and the driller. The drill floor is located directly under the derrick. The floor is a relatively small work area in which the rig crew conducts operations, usually adding or removing drill pipe to or from the drill string. The rig floor is the most dangerous location on the rig because heavy iron is moved around there. Drill string connections are made or broken on the drill floor, and the driller's console for controlling the major components of the rig is located there. Attached to the rig floor is a small metal room, the doghouse, where the rig crew can meet, take breaks and take refuge from the elements during idle times.

Drill Bit

A drill bit is a tool designed to produce a generally cylindrical hole (wellbore) in the earth's crust by the rotary drilling method for the discovery and extraction of hydrocarbons such as crude oil and natural gas. This type of tool is alternately referred to as a rock bit, or simply a bit. The hole diameter produced by drill bits is quite small, from about 3.5 inches (8.9 cm) to 30 inches (76 cm), compared to the depth of the hole, which can range from 1,000 feet (300 m) to more than 30,000 feet (9,100 m). Subsurface formations are broken apart mechanically by cutting elements of the bit by scraping, grinding or localized compressive fracturing. The cuttings produced by the bit are most typically removed from the wellbore and continuously returned to the surface by the method of direct circulation.

Monkey Board

The monkey board is 90 ft up from the rotary table where the derrickman stands and around 30 ft below the crown block, located at the top of the derrick. The derrickman racks back stands of drill collars, heavy weight pipe and drill pipe into steel fingers ready to be run back in the hole when required.

Crown Block

A crown block is the stationary section of a block and tackle that contains a set of pulleys or sheaves through which the drill line (wire rope) is threaded or reeved and is opposite and above the travelling block. The combination of the travelling block, crown block and wire rope drill line gives the ability to lift weights in the hundreds of thousands of pounds. On larger drilling rigs, when raising and lowering the derrick, line tensions over a million pounds are not unusual.

Blowout Preventer

A blowout preventer (BOP) (pronounced B-O-P, not 'bop') is a specialized valve or similar mechanical device, used to seal, control and monitor oil and gas wells to prevent blowouts, the uncontrolled release of crude oil or natural gas from a well. They are usually installed in stacks of other valves.

Blowout preventers were developed to cope with extreme erratic pressures and uncontrolled flow (formation kick) emanating from a well reservoir during drilling. Kicks can lead to a potentially catastrophic event known as a blowout. In addition to controlling the downhole (occurring in the drilled hole) pressure and the flow of oil and gas, blowout preventers are intended to prevent tubing (e.g. drill pipe and well casing), tools and drilling fluid from being blown out of the wellbore (also known as bore hole, the hole leading to the reservoir) when a blowout threatens.

Blowout preventers are critical to the safety of crew, rig (the equipment system used to drill a wellbore) and environment, and to the monitoring and maintenance of well integrity; thus blowout preventers are intended to provide fail-safety to the systems that include them.

Shale Shaker

Shale shakers are components of drilling equipment used in many industries, such as coal cleaning, mining, oil and gas drilling. They are the first phase of a solids control system on a drilling rig and are used to remove large solids (cuttings) from the drilling fluid ('mud'). Drilling fluids are integral to the drilling process and, among other functions, serve to lubricate and cool the drill bit as well as convey the drilled cuttings away from the bore hole. These fluids are a mixture of various chemicals in a water or oil-based solution and can be very expensive to make. For both environmental reasons and to reduce the cost of drilling operations, drilling fluid losses are minimized by stripping them away from the drilled cuttings before the cuttings are disposed of. This is done using a multitude of specialized machines and tanks.

Shale shakers are the primary solids separation tool on a rig. After returning to the surface of the well the used drilling fluid flows directly to the shale shakers where it begins to be processed. Once processed by the shale shakers the drilling fluid is deposited into the mud tanks where other solid control equipment begin to remove the finer solids from it. The solids removed by the shale shaker are discharged out of the discharge port into a separate holding tank where they await further treatment or disposal.

Shale shakers are considered by most of the drilling industry to be the most important device in the solid control system as the performance of the successive equipment directly relates to the cleanliness of the treated drilling fluid.

Mud Pump

A mud pump (sometimes referred to as a mud drilling pump or drilling mud pump), is a reciprocating piston/plunger pump designed to circulate drilling fluid under high pressure (up to 7,500 psi or 52,000 kPa) down the drill string and back up the annulus. A mud pump is an important part of the equipment used for oil well drilling.

Casing Equipment

Casing equipment will make up casing 30" down to 23/8" tubing, utilising a selection of hydraulic power tongs sizes each attached to a hydraulic power unit by hi pressure hydraulic rubber hoses. The casing is held by jaws in the tong that enable the casing to be turned clock wise to make the pin end connection into the female box connection. A torque gauge is attached to a back-up line from the tong to a back-up post located on the rig floor and the operator can monitor how much torque the connection requires. Different types and sizes of elevators are used to lift and hold the pipe while the casing is lowered or pulled from the well. Premium casing/tubing connections are run utilizing a torque turn computer attached to the power tong back-up-line and monitors both torque and turns of the pipe make-up.

Appendix 3:
Oilfield Equipment Diagrams

 platform

 Semisub

 Drillship

 Jack-up

 Tender Semisub

 Land Rig

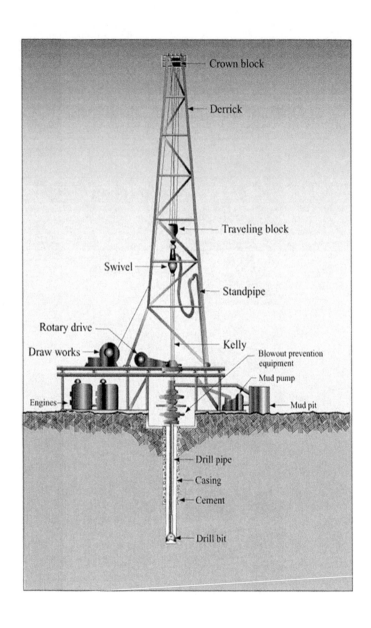

Crown block

Derrick

Traveling block

Swivel

Standpipe

Rotary drive

Kelly

Draw works

Blowout prevention
equipment

Mud pump

Engines

Mud pit

Drill pipe

Casing

Cement

Drill bit

HYDRALIC POWER UNIT

CASING POWER TONG

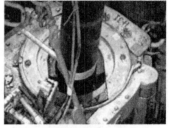

CASING STABBER

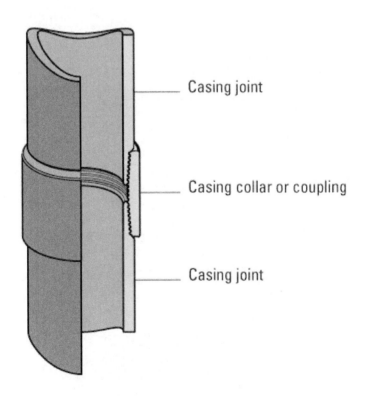

Casing joint

Casing collar or coupling

Casing joint

OILWELL CEMENTATION

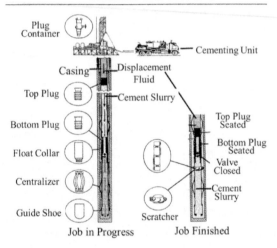

Plug Container

Cementing Unit

Casing — Displacement Fluid

Top Plug — Cement Slurry

Bottom Plug

Float Collar

Centralizer

Guide Shoe

Scratcher

Job in Progress

Top Plug Seated

Bottom Plug Seated

Valve Closed

Cement Slurry

Job Finished

CASING CENTRALIZERS   FLOAT SHOE - FLOAT COLLAR

Acknowledgements

Mariann Johansen-Ellis, for standing by me for the last 25 years and for being my first true love.

Hadyn Ellis always looked out for me and got me started in the oilfield.

David Ellis was instrumental in sorting out a lot of problems for me and taking an interest in where I was and what I was doing.

John Ellis, my younger brother and only surviving sibling, pushed by me to follow in my footsteps but could not bear leaving home for this nomadic life.

Ellie Ross, for always reassuring me that I could do it.

Dave Piper, for getting me past the finishing post without cracking up.

All my friends and colleagues in the oil industry, who helped me along this exciting journey.

Alison Thompson, The Proof Fairy, for doing such a great job sorting through my dyslexic mumbo jumbo of a manuscript.

Printed in Great Britain
by Amazon

86966800R00142